DIZZY IN KARACHI:
A JOURNEY TO PAKISTAN

MALIHA MASOOD

Booktrope Editions
Seattle WA 2013

Cover Design by Greg Simanson

Author's Note:
*This work is based on my travels to Pakistan from May – October 2003. It
conveys my impressions of people and places as I experienced them during
that time. To protect their privacy, some of the character names have been
altered. All cultural, religious, historical, and political references are my
own conclusions. In the case of inadvertent factual inaccuracies, the fault is
entirely mine.*

PRINT ISBN 978-1-935961-99-4
EPUB ISBN 978-1-62015-103-7

For further information regarding permissions, please contact
info@booktrope.com.

Library of Congress Control Number: 2013931534

For my parents and my son

and

in memory of Dadijan

ALSO BY MALIHA MASOOD

Zaatar Days Henna Nights: Adventures, Dreams and Destinations Across the Middle East

I'm everything you lost. You won't forgive me.
My memory keeps getting in the way of your history.
There is nothing to forgive. You won't forgive me.
There is everything to forgive. You can't forgive me.
If only somehow you could have been mine,
what would not have been possible in the world?

—*Agha Shahid Ali*

CONTENTS

1
BREAKING FRONTIERS

Khyber Pass, May 2003

THE BAZAAR IN LANDI KOTAL is a gunsmith's paradise. An impressive display of Kalashnikovs and AK-47's, pistols and hand grenades. I ask one of the merchants if he still has the Stinger missiles that the CIA supplied to the Afghan Mujahideen resistance.

"They were brave men," he says. "They fight Russians for USA."

A nasty cough ripples from his lungs and then the merchant draws my attention to an authentic Chinese assault rifle. Would I care to see the famous Israeli Uzi sub machine gun? He also has some old Enfield .303 rifles.

I lead him back to the question of Stingers, many of which were unused after the Soviet withdrawal. The United States government had spent vast amounts of time and money to recover the surface to air missiles, but the covert nature and lack of oversight of arms shipments made it virtually impossible to keep track of what happened once the weapons left American hands and were funneled into Pakistan.

"My friend in Dara," says the old merchant. "He have. Many people buy to fight war in Kashmir."

I turn down his request to see his collection of revolvers. Apparently, he's quite proud of the local knockoffs of the .32 caliber Webley. They're made by a factory in Peshawar, where you can also buy top quality hashish. He can get me some smuggled stash from yet another friend.

Landi Kotal is an old garrison town, dating back to the days of the Raj. Crumbling watchtowers and insignias of various British regiments still guard this highest point on the Khyber Pass. We drive slowly through the cantonment, past the barracks and the Khyber rifles mess.

"Here we are," says Anwar and pulls into a long driveway. He salutes the approaching servants. Some of them are barefoot.

"Hungry?" Anwar turns to me and smiles politely.

I have no idea where we are, but I gather it's some kind of a guesthouse or a lodge though there are no signs of any other visitors given the empty lot. My stomach is making all kinds of strange noises, partly from hunger, partly from the dread of not knowing what kind of a situation I have gotten myself into. I barely know this Anwar guy who is a friend of a friend I knew no better. But something made me trust these people and so here I am on top of the Khyber Pass about to eat lunch.

"Famished!" I reply and smile back.

The lobby is decorated with ethnic handicrafts and black and white photographs of former guests. I recognize some illustrious faces. Prince Charles, Nehru, Jinnah, the Malaysian Prime Minister Mahatir.

"This way," Anwar extends a hand and ushers me into the dining room.

We settle down to a hearty lunch of lentils, flatbread, okra and mutton rice strongly flavored with cardamom. The dishes arrive one by one in gleaming stainless steel. *Daal, chappati, bhindi, biryani.*

The Pashtun wait staff hover around Anwar and I, clearly not accustomed to serving such inferior company. The two of us are sitting at one end of a huge wooden table that can accommodate at least twenty. Anwar eats quickly and elapses into an awkward silence while eyeing me furtively in between mouthfuls. His discomfort makes me tongue tied so we both end up saying nothing for the better part of the meal. I wonder what's in store afterwards. Anwar hasn't hammered out much of a plan. He doesn't strike me as the planning sort given this impromptu Saturday afternoon excursion.

Just a little drive, Anwar had called it when we stepped outside his Peshawar bungalow where I have been staying as a house guest with Anwar's family. That he was a family man was the only thing I did learn about Anwar before preying on his hospitality. Plus the fact that he worked at the local post office. That sounded nice. I was desperate for a little adventure. Islamabad was getting to be quite a bore. So I went through my contact list and somehow things fell into place. Just a little drive. He was being far too modest.

Imagine a moonscape of biscuit colored hills. It felt as if I was airborne, witnessing sharp angles of earth and sky. The road hugged a series of tight switchbacks. In the back of a Land Rover, I kept sliding from left to right on the vinyl seat like a stray hockey puck. Visions of invaders and conquests danced through my head. The Great Alexander, Mahmud of Ghaznavi, Genghis Khan. Men, armor, horses. They were all here.

According to the local newspapers, Pakistani paratroopers were battling Taliban militants all along the border between Pakistan and Afghanistan. The Khyber functions as the only land route between the two countries. It is arguably the world's most notorious pass. I hadn't really had the time to conceive of all the dangers involved, of the thousand and one things that could go wrong. The whole excursion had been so spontaneous and effortless, like something too good to be real. My mind was full of questions, but I went along the drive, unable to stop its momentum. As we entered the Federally Administered Tribal Areas, better known as FATA, Anwar drove under a large white banner that struck a more sinister note. *No foreigners allowed beyond this point.*

Thanks to my Pakistani passport, a Political Agent had kindly given me permission to travel through.

A Political Agent. Khyber Pass. The Tribal Areas. This I couldn't wait to see.

The road got steeper and curvier. We saw a man pedaling furiously on a bicycle with three more trailing behind. Anwar pointed out the cycle smugglers who were paid two hundred rupees for each Chinese manufactured bike they transported from the Afghan border into Peshawar, a distance of roughly sixty harrowing miles. It was a thankless job, risking flat tires, head on collisions and avalanches on an average day's work. But the profit margin was huge fetching as much as three thousand rupees for every smuggled bike sold in the Rawalpindi bazaar.

"Lookout!" I screamed.

One of the cyclists had brazenly overtaken us around a sharp bend. Anwar beeped and shouted some choice profanities in Punjabi and Urdu. It was rather unnecessary.

I had heard about the rampant corruption along the Khyber. Imported goods shipped from Singapore, Malaysia, Japan to Karachi port were loaded onto trucks for transshipment to Kabul, about a thousand miles away. Upon reaching the Afghan border, the refrigerators, air conditioners and television sets were unloaded and smuggled back into Pakistan. At every checkpoint, bribes substituted for customs duty. Prosperous smugglers and drug barons had built huge villas just outside of Peshawar, complete with manicured gardens, marble entry halls and a private militia of armed bodyguards.

When I asked Anwar if he approved of all this, he simply shrugged his shoulders. Then he expounded on his pet theory that the Tribal Areas was one of the safer parts of Pakistan. The lack of rigid laws gave less incentive to break laws. Justice was a private concern. For the most part, people were just trying to get by, making a living the best way they could, even if meant selling drugs and weapons.

*　*　*

"Afghanistan is waiting!"

I am staring at a tall, dark-skinned man with a mile long grin.

"*Tayar ho?*"

He asks if I'm ready to go.

Soon after lunch, I meet Ghafoor Shah, the local Political Agent who has allowed me to come this far. We sit down for some tea and lemon cookies in the garden. I want to ask Ghafoor about his job, but he keeps teasing me about my low intake of sugar and dumps three heaping spoonfuls into my chai.

"You need to put on some weight," he declares. "How can you climb mountains looking like that?"

Ghafoor is probably in his mid thirties though he looks much older. Clear hazel eyes radiate warmth, making the rest of his heavy-set features less foreboding. I like the way he laughs, rocking back and forth and clutching his stomach. His easygoing manner immediately strikes a friendly chord. Ghafoor recounts his adventures in Chitral. I can almost picture tiny exclamation points dancing in his pupils.

"The Kalash are a very interesting people," says Ghafoor. "They did not convert to Islam, but they are good kind people, better than most Muslims! And you should see the women. They have long long hair up to here," he touches his hips. "And they wear shells in their braids, like your native American Indians."

"Are you sure about that?" I ask. "I thought they wore feathers. I don't remember any shells."

"Shells, feathers, it is all the same!"

"So will you take me to Chitral?"

"Well, you'd better fatten up those skinny shoulders first!"

Ghafoor laughs and dumps more sugar in my cold tea.

I try to include Anwar in the conversation, but he sits in a corner and sulks, unable to compete with Ghafoor's easy banter. All of a sudden, my newfound acquaintance stands up and punches some numbers on his cell phone. The conversation is short and swift.

"Excuse me, but I have to go extend a ceasefire," announces Ghafoor with a grave expression.

I ask the Political Agent what he'll offer as incentives.

"Oh you know, the usual carrot and stick approach!"

Twenty minutes later, Ghafoor is back in the garden. We take his jeep and drive further up the Khyber Pass towards the Afghan border. Ghafoor's three bodyguards trail behind in a separate jeep. More dusty barren streets and gun toting bazaars come into view. Children in tattered clothes wave to us and try to keep up with our vehicle. Some give up quickly and run away towards a row of mud brick huts. The bolder ones are quite persistent before they finally quit and I watch them shrinking in the distance getting smaller and smaller until they are out of sight. I glance through the side view mirror at Ghafoor. He looks rather smug. The ceasefire deal must have gone well.

We pass a truck whose entire body has been painted with images of dusky eyed maidens, flying partridges, waterfalls and snow capped meadows mingled with Quranic verses to ward off the evil eye. The vibrant colors and bold, bright brushstrokes remind me of Gaugin.

"Border patrol!" chimes Ghafoor. "Hide your weapons!"

He slams on the brakes and we sit in a massive traffic snarl leading up to the Pakistani/Afghan border at Torkham. More and more trucks are slowing down awaiting inspection at the checkpoint just ahead. Forty five minutes later, we pull over to a stop in a barren compound near the border gate. I expect to see a steady flow of human traffic, but there is hardly anyone about. After the 1979 Soviet invasion of Afghanistan, Pakistan absorbed over three million Afghan refugees. Along with the poor families and conservative minded tribes came an entire generation hardened by war. They brought into Pakistan a potent brew of militancy and Islam with disastrous consequences.

December 1979. I am obsessed with this date. Because like all seminal dates, it changed history and forever altered the face of Pakistan. Much of what is wrong with the country today can be traced back to the events that followed.

If only things could have been different. If only the United States had used its own manpower to kick the Soviets out of Afghanistan instead of relying on local recruits. If only Pakistan had not been in the grip of an ambitious military ruler desperate to consolidate power and legitimize his authority. If only Afghanistan had been an island without porous borders. If only the Soviets were less pig headed. If only.

Like any ably minded politician, General Zia ul Haq smelled Opportunity when the United States requested help to ward off the Communist threat next door. Zia's agenda and that of the U.S. became one and the same--to radicalize Pakistan with religion in order to mobilize support for the anti-Soviet insurgency in Afghanistan. The CIA funded thousands of training camps in Pakistan and beyond for the *mujahideen* resistance fighters. General Zia's cooperation with the Americans made him quite a hero in the West. Once the Soviets were kicked out, Afghanistan was left to fend for itself. And so was Pakistan. Relations between Islamabad and Washington got more and more strained. When the Carter administration offered a $400 million aid package multi million to alleviate the Afghan refugee situation, Zia dismissed it as peanuts.

Perhaps he ought to have replied with a two-part question that would be answered in due time. *Who was more in need of the other? And which one of us got the short end of the stick?*

We stop at the customs building and pile into a stuffy room overlooking the border post. Ghafoor insists we have more chai. He gestures for me to join him outside. The three bodyguards spring to life, trailing us at a modest distance, Kalashnikovs in hand, and nozzles pointing downwards.

"Don't worry about a thing," Ghafoor says. *"Yahan, meri hukumat hay!"*

This is my turf he assures with a sweep of his hand. I take out my camera that I've been carrying underneath my shawl and aim it towards the Welcome to Pakistan sign that shares a billboard with Khyber Rifles and Pepsi. The trucks keep piling up at the border checkpoint. Not allowed to go past the gate, I cross a narrow ridge over a gully and sink my feet into Afghan soil.

Ghafoor grins and points to my flimsy sandals. "Is that what you climb mountains in?"

I inscribe our names in Urdu on the gravelly earth with the back of my chewed up Biro.

Just in time for sunset, Ghafoor decides to take us up to a TV tower, sensing my need to prolong the adventure. "There is a fantastic view of Afghanistan from the summit," he says. "But I don't think you are fit enough to climb all the way up!"

I stick out my tongue in retaliation. We pile back into his jeep. I am sandwiched between Ghafoor who drives and Anwar who is chain smoking Marlboros. Each time Ghafoor shifts gears, his hand digs into my waist and I cry aloud in fake torment that causes him to double over in laughter. The jeep lurches forward, tracing the curve of an unpaved dirt road. I watch the angle of the sky shifting at every turn, just like in an airplane.

The TV tower perches up a steep incline. Fierce winds flap against my chador as I walk along the edge of a cliff. Honey colored hills spread out in all directions, making me forget the concept of flat land. Peering towards the horizon, I can only make out the faint outlines of bluish mountain ranges in the disappearing light. From this vantage point, Afghanistan looks serene and beautiful as if newly born and it is difficult to imagine the actual horror and destruction of the war torn country that lies beyond.

Ghafoor's bodyguards squat on their haunches smoking *bedis*. Their Kalashnikovs are resting on the ground. I am tempted to hold one just to see what it feels like. One of the guards sees me eying his rifle. He gestures me to come forward and then he picks up the weapon and cradles it in my arms like a precious infant. It's lighter than I had expected. No more than ten or twelve pounds. I adjust my head scarf to cover my face and aim towards Kabul, while my onlookers laugh and urge me to find Osama Bin Laden.

"You'll be a rich lady if you find Osama," says Ghafoor in a perfectly serious tone. "And if we find him together, we'll split the proceeds, fifty-fifty."

"Come," he adds and looks up at the darkening sky. "It is time for *maghrib* prayers."

We rub our fingers into the parched brown earth and pat them over our faces, arms and feet for the ritual ablutions. The lack of water necessitates sand as our cleanser. A couple of jute rugs are spread out in the direction of Mecca. Maybe not so far away, Osama is praying in some cave. What possible connection do we have as Muslims?

"*Allahu Akbar.*"

We proclaim the glory of God and bend at the knees.

"*Allahu Akbar.*"

We submit our will to the Almighty and touch foreheads to the ground.

"*Allahu Akbar.*"

We surrender before the Creator and sit in silence.

A girl from America in search of her roots, a kindly bureaucrat who drinks too much tea and the world's most wanted criminal – all of us praying, the rite of *namaz*, united in time by our actions, but in our minds, we may as well be galaxies apart.

*   *   *

You can tell a lot about a person by the way he or she shakes your hand. Typically, in Pakistan, men and women do not shake hands, except in business settings or in hip young circles. I often made the mistake of extending my hand in greeting to which I received at best a wishy washy grazing of palms or sometimes a total lack of acknowledgement. Even among women, the handshake was often nothing more than a loose hand hold. There was no actual shaking or pumping. Your hands would meet but they would not move. The whole gesture felt fake and unnatural. It made both parties uncomfortable.

So when Ghafoor takes my right hand and pumps it firmly to say goodbye, I know right away why we hit it off. His handshake is sincere and honest. It seals our friendship. Ghafoor gives me his card inscribed with a quaint job title. *Tehsildar.* Village Administrator. We exchange email addresses and phone numbers, planning to meet up next time he comes down to Islamabad.

Anwar and I head back to Peshawar, winding our way down the Khyber Pass in near darkness, with the headlights of the Land Rover car guiding the way ahead. Only the wail of the Pashtun song on the radio keeps my thoughts from drifting. I keep thinking of that exceptionally warm handshake, the kind I had never before received in Pakistan.

PAKISTAN.

Just the mention of the word triggers a flurry of emotions and contradictions.

Pakistan: You are horror stories in the media, mayhem and violence spewing cyclones of terror.

Pakistan: You are so very old and cultured with layers upon layers of history.

Pakistan: You are fragments of my childhood floating in my mind like confetti.

Pakistan: You are my remembrance and my ignorance, my pride as well as my shame.

I had come back to explore all of the above. But it was impossible to know at this early stage how the journey would pan out and whether or not I could travel freely through the country despite all its hazards. It was obviously going to be a challenge. Pakistan was certainly not a tourist destination. There were far more tourists in Greenland. And after 9/11, what little cache Pakistan possessed on the tourist map had sunk Titanic-like way beneath the modern traveler's horizon.

It was a pity. A hundred years earlier, when Pakistan was not even born, the region we now call Pakistan was part of the British Empire and Europeans were stampeding all over the place in all manners and styles. There were merchants from the East India Trading Company doing business in the Bengal, army officers attending fancy balls in Karachi's cantonment, intrepid mountaineers mapping the Himalayan and Karakoram mountain passes, their hardships unaided by Gore-Tex and high tech fleece.

These days, the Gore-Tex and fleece folks were not so prominent. There might be a hardy handful launching summit expeditions to K-2 sponsored by various foreign governments and foundations. They were financially secured, goal oriented and highly driven. There were no more casual visitors to the country. Every foreigner that made it to Pakistan had a strong sense of purpose. Tackling mountains and saving the country was high on the list. These intentions were good, but you saw only what you wanted to see, leaving behind so much more to be discovered and understood.

Just three weeks earlier, I had been roaming the streets of Boston on a glorious spring day, exhilarated to be done with final exams and even more exhilarated with the thought of returning to my birthplace after twenty one years. It was going to be my first trip back since leaving Karachi and immigrating to America in 1982. I was eleven years old at the time, too young to feel the ache of exile, but old enough to know that my life would be irrevocably transformed by that move.

Growing up between two homelands muddled my sense of belonging. I was hoping that my journey to Pakistan would allow me to resume a long suspended dialogue with the country and discover once and for all what it means to me after all this time away. I needed to merge the Pakistan I had known and loved as a child where you could ride camels on the beach and eat fresh roasted peanuts wrapped in newspaper cones with newer, harsher realities, where you could get killed in a bomb blast or a road side shooting simply because you were heading to the beach at the wrong time of day.

I knew that the Pakistan I would be returning to as an adult was no longer the Pakistan I had abandoned as a child. The place had changed so much and so had I. The girl that used to recite flowery verses by Wordsworth in a sing song British accent was long gone. Nowadays, she was much more likely to quote Noam Chomsky as a free thinking American citizen. My allegiance was split across two different nations as different as oil and water. Which was my home? Where did I truly belong?

These were not easy questions. But I needed some answers and I needed them now. If I waited any longer, Pakistan and I would drift apart forever, the chasm between us too insurmountable to bridge. So I did what had to be done and booked a Virgin Air flight departing from Logan airport to Islamabad in May of 2003. My plan was to live in Pakistan for the next five months and to travel the length and breadth of the country, although I was clueless about the precise wheres and hows of such endeavors.

You're making a colossal blunder screamed my ever practical head. This whole expedition has disaster written all over it. Indeed, in the weeks preceding my departure, there was talk of US armed forces preparing to invade Iraq. The whole world appeared to be going mad and there I was traipsing off to one of the world's most dangerous countries to do some root searching.

Crazy place to go was the attitude of the security mavens on campus.

You go girl cheered the globetrotters.

Do not tell them you're American, advised one friend.

Do not tell them you're Pakistani, advised another.

By all means go, and while you're there, try to beat some sense into those thick Pakistani skulls was the advice from a trusted professor who seemed to think I was in for a very intriguing summer.

My father's reaction was less enthusiastic. He pointed out the State Department's travel advisory against Pakistan and urged me to come back to my senses.

"I don't know what you're trying to prove," Abboo had said on the phone from Seattle. "There's nothing to see there anymore."

You have to go back. You must do this.

"You're bound to be disappointed," my father continued. "Don't say I didn't warn you."

Do not be afraid. It will all work out. Inshallah.

I listened to my heart and moved forward.

Days before my departure, I tried to do some travel research on Pakistan and came up with some pretty sorry results. There were no decent guidebooks other than some dated Lonely Planet copies on mountaineering. I wasn't sure I'd need the services of local Sherpas. The public library turned up a few quaint travelogues published over sixty years ago featuring the trials and tribulations of eccentric Englishmen roaming through the tribal hinterlands braving fierce warlords and village chieftains. They might come in handy if only I could have disguised myself as an eccentric Englishman.

What would be more useful were the hefty current affairs tomes on prominent display at Barnes and Noble. Their titles were not very inventive. You could boil them all down to the likes of Allah's soldiers or stormy Jihads. I was doubtful how much more I needed to know about the world's foremost terror den and its bearded militants chanting death to America. Seldom were such images balanced by alternative images of ordinary life in Pakistan.

It is to be expected. Even in its accuracy news tends to be skewed because it only highlights the horror stories. The good stuff gets ignored simply because it is not newsworthy. When it comes to Pakistan, there was far more bad than good. In fact, the place seems to have some kind of self destructive talent for producing bad fare which makes us fearful and suspicious and justifiably so. But you can't understand a country solely through its problems.

Of course, there is a deeper obstacle to discovering Pakistan. The place simply does not exist. If it does, it is like a fractured vase, each piece as varied and distinct as the hand holding it. Pakistan's very creation was the result of a fracture, of breakage and division. How can such an entity ever be seen as a whole?

Time and again, I would look at Pakistan on a world map and trace its shape with my index finger. I longed to feel a beat, a pulse, any movement that would immerse me into this fabric at once familiar and strange.

2

A Bubble in the Hills

Islamabad, May 2003

I WISH THE BEAUTY QUEEN WOULD GET UP and let me have my turn. She lies on her back at the foot of the bed with her lips pressed, her long hair spilling over the edge of the mattress as a woman kneels beside the bed with thread in her mouth--some of which unspools and wraps between her outstretched hands--to deftly sculpt Momina's eyebrows into exquisite half moons. I had left the office early and hurried back to the dorm by four thirty counting on what Beenish had told me in the morning over breakfast as she wrapped two stale *aloo parathas* in a newspaper for my lunch.

"Waxing lady coming today. Don't be late."

I remove the sweaty *dupatta* coiled around my neck and try to engage Seher in a conversation. "Busy day at school?"

"Hmmm," she murmurs as her fingers dance a jig on her cell phone texting madly.

Someone kicks the air conditioner and it hums back to life. I straighten out the bundle of newspapers on my nightstand and try to read an article, but I can't get into it. My pink highlighter is missing. I scan the bedroom and try to figure out which of my roommates has the guiltiest expression. But no one is looking in my direction. As far as these girls are concerned, I'm a nonentity, a person of no consequence to their busy collegiate lives. Like a speck of dust or a cobweb, I'm something to put up with, tolerate, and basically ignore.

It's not so bothersome, now that I've been here for a few weeks and settled into a routine, but just the same, I would like to be treated as more than just a speck of dust or a cobweb. After all, it has been over two decades since I was last in Pakistan. Surely I deserve a better reception than this.

"No way!!" Tahira hollers from her perch by the computer. "You guys! Come check this out."

Everyone except for Momina goes over to the flickering screen to see some Bollywood dance video. Tahira turns up the volume so we can all hear the upbeat song. It's a new number that I'm totally unfamiliar with. But I can understand the Hindi/Urdu lyrics and despite my crummy mood, I find myself humming along to the melody as I change into a fresh pair of *shalwar-kameez* and make a beeline for Momina's bed.

Momina. What to say about her that hasn't already been said before about the beauty queens of this world. I'll start with the obvious. Smoky green eyes. Glossy mahogany locks. Rosy alabaster complexion. Tall and slender. Curves in all the right places. Regal in her bearing. Haughty and charming. As soon as I had laid eyes on her, I had pictured her on the cover of French Vogue. Of course, Momina had scarcely said hi to me. It didn't help matters that we had gotten off to a bad start because I had hogged the communal closet that we all shared and taken up too many shelves with my stuff. Momina had barged into our room lugging a giant suitcase and yanked open the double doors of an old teak armoire.

"Now where am I to put my clothes?" she had complained in a lilting Indo-British accent with one hand on her hip. "Who has taken up all this space?"

She wore fashionable jeans. Bootleg cut in a dark indigo wash. And tortoise shell glasses, rectangular and oversized. They made the Beauty Queen look even sexier.

The room is starting to smell of burnt sugar and something citrusy. The waxing lady places an aluminum sauce pan on the nightstand and begins to plaster Momina's legs with sticky brown paste. Now I'm really ticked off. It's so like Momina to monopolize the woman's time. She's been at it for over an hour since I got here and is clearly taking her time what with all that chattering and giggling with Momina who must be her favorite client. Even if I declare that I'm next in line, it would make no difference. Momina would still bully me. She knows she can get away with it. A face like that could melt the heart of an ax-murderer.

"My turn!"

Seher slouches in a chair with her head aimed at the ceiling. The waxing lady starts threading Seher's caterpillar eyebrows. I glance towards Momina. She's sitting on the floor, leaning against my bed and painting her toenails. I have half a mind to swing my legs down and upset the scarlet red bottle dangerously close to her Nokia just because I can't stand its ring tone.

"Want to go to the mall tomorrow?"

The Beauty Queen looks at me inquiringly. I know that she still sees me as that thirty something oddball from America who hasn't quite gotten the hang of this place. It would be useless to explain anything to the contrary. My anger is starting to cool off. It's hard to stay mad at Momina. She flashes her angelic smile. I shrug defeat and change for dinner.

*   *   *

"Aunty thinks you're a spy," Tahira blurts out.

She's peering as usual at her computer screen which looks bigger than its normal size in the sun's vicious glare. I've been enjoying the peace and quiet in our room, reading my guidebook on a Saturday afternoon and listening to Tahira's soft taps on her keyboard.

"What are you talking about?" I mumble with my eyes peeled on the book.

"She's convinced you're with the CIA," Tahira responds. "Are you?"

"What??!"

I snap my book shut and sit up straighter trying to think what on earth would make Aunty reach a conclusion so outlandish. She had been asking me a lot of questions lately, inviting me to her downstairs quarters every Sunday for some afternoon tea that basically gave her the opportunity to stage an inquisition that was quite intrusive even by Pakistani standards.

I was expecting the usual *why are you still single, when will you get married and how many children do you plan to have*. I was not expecting *by what mode of transport did you arrive in the country, what is the nature of your work in Islamabad, and do you have any local contacts*.

When I bring this up with Tahira, she thinks it makes perfect sense. I'm from America. I'm living undercover in Pakistan at a college dormitory so I can learn the culture as an insider. I blend in by wearing local clothes even though my *shalwar-kameez* outfits are hopelessly out of date. I speak Urdu albeit with a heavy accent audible to everyone's ears except mine. I have two passports, American and Pakistani. The American passport has stamps from all over the world, including some recent ones from the Middle East. The Pakistani passport has been newly issued from the New York Consulate.

Could I look any more suspicious? Aunty is sure to launch her own private investigation. She's bound to find out sooner or later that I'm a CIA agent. But don't worry. My secret is safe for now. Tahira will alert the girls. They won't breathe a word. As long as I raid the supply closet at work and bring them some mechanical pencils for their homework. They're good for drawing flowcharts and writing equations. Exams are coming up. Mechanical Engineering is going to be brutal. Comp Sci is easier. They're learning binary search algorithms. Some of them already know Java and Oracle.

"Six thousand Rupees," Aunty had replied three weeks earlier when I inquired about the cost of staying at her place. I paid her on the spot the very modest equivalent of one hundred greenbacks. It was the monthly rate per head for full board and meals. Then Aunty went over the rules that would make any convent proud. No visits from members of the opposite sex, curfew after eleven PM and limited phone calls between two and five PM when Aunty and her daughters took their siestas.

So this was how it would turn out. I had come all the way back to Pakistan after twenty one years to enact my very own *Fawlty Towers* episode. Aunty had offered a flimsy handshake and a tight lipped smile. I was ushered toward a spiral staircase.

"Your room is the first on the right," Aunty said. "You will share with Tahira, Momina, Seher and Bushra."

I gave a weak nod.

"Very nice Pakistani girls," Aunty added. "From good families."

A frail looking girl in a yellow cotton *shalwar-kameez* approached us and handed Aunty a cordless phone.

"Thank you Beenish."

Aunty took the phone into the formal sitting room.

The girl and I looked at each other. She was about my height, maybe an inch or two taller, but so thin and pale faced.

"Hullo," she piped and giggled like a child. "The others are watching TV."

I followed Beenish upstairs into what looked like a girls dorm lounge outfitted with a hideous lime green plaid sofa and several plastic chairs. No one paid any attention to me. I chose to focus on the show which was some kind of a matchmaking program, basically the local version of the Dating Game, called *Shadi Online*. Someone snickered when a nervous contestant asked about her future mother-in-law. Was she the bossy type?

"This is so boring!"

A girl with long black hair tied up in a ponytail switched the channel to *MTV Asia*. It featured an old Madonna song. *Lucky Star*.

"Double boring!!"

"Come on, *yaar*! Find something decent."

There were some rapid clicks on the remote. They settled on a talk show with a transvestite host.

It had been a peaceful morning. I got up at dawn to read and write in my journal and I even managed to wash my clothes with a bar of soap in the bathroom sink while it was still clean and accessible. Beenish had made me a cup of strong black tea, rich and creamy with condensed milk and just a spoonful of sugar. I took it with me on the terrace as I hung my laundry on a fraying jute rope. I couldn't remember the last time I had hand washed my clothes, and I found some pleasure in the work, rinsing the soapy water, squeezing out all the excess moisture from the garments and piling their cold wet slabs in a bucket.

The terrace overlooks a small garden with large, bright pink Hibiscus flower bushes and an old *neem* tree that reminds me of the kind we had in the front lawn of our old Saddar house in Karachi.

My mother used to crush its leaves and put them in my bath as a disinfectant, after I had contracted chicken pox. It was an ancient Ayurvedic treatment.

Right and left of the garden are the adjoining houses in F-8, one of the older neighborhoods of Islamabad. My newfound residence is not really a dorm. It's a private home, whose upstairs portion has been converted into a makeshift collegiate dormitory with four spacious bedrooms, two full bathrooms down the hallway, a common room equipped with a flat screen TV and a Sony boom box that always gets a workout when my roommates are doing their ironing. There is also a kitchen, but it goes unused since Beenish does all the cooking in the larger and more comfortable one downstairs next to the formal dining room where she serves breakfast, lunch, afternoon tea and dinner to twenty hungry mouths every single day.

Beenish is all of fifteen years old. And she works like a slave. How does she do it, I wonder time and again. How does she remain so cheerful and happy? Her eyes are always glowing and smiling at me with some kind of an inner light.

*   *   *

Islamabad is my entry point into Pakistan. I have come here to work as a summer intern at an international think tank. It was important to have a comfortable landing pad after a hiatus of twenty one years. So I opted for a job with a well defined nine to five schedule to channel my energy. My goal was to stay busy and focused instead of dithering around like a lost soul as I had done on previous treks around the world. Along with a routine, I needed a respectable cover for my presence in Pakistan.

The homecoming aspect was nebulous and rather touchy. I didn't want to blab about it in public and be taken for a sentimental fool. If I told people that I simply wanted to travel, I would be the source of endless jokes and laughter. No sane woman would dare travel alone in Pakistan unless she didn't know any better. The Khyber trip was an extremely lucky break. I was hoping there would be more such weekend escapades, but I still had to have a home base where I was doing something useful.

Research Assistant. I could live with that.

The thing I'm researching is President Musharraf's Devolution Plan. It's a rather pretentious title for the grassroots democratization program that became a top priority in the wake of the October 1999 coup that brought the General to power. Every morning, I scan the national papers for the Local Bodies election results, where city magistrates, known as *nazims* are allegedly exercising people power. One of the main tenets of Musharraf's plan is to undermine federalism by ignoring constitutional safeguards designed to protect Pakistan's provincial autonomy. This ends up tightening control between local governance and the power brokers at the center, making the *nazims* token figure heads devoid of any real political, legislative or fiscal responsibilities. In other words, the Dev Plan is basically an acceptable rationale to bolster legitimacy for military intervention under the guise of local governance.

Successive authoritarian regimes in Pakistan had instituted similar schemes, starting with Ayub Khan's Basic Democracy Plan in 1959. Aiming to neutralize demands for democracy, Ayub relied on an indirect system of governance where local councilors known as basic democrats were appointed to run local provincial affairs. They initially numbered at 80,000 and increased to 120,000 conveniently doubling as an Electoral College vote bank for the president. The plan did nothing to resolve Pakistan's age-old problem of power sharing between the central government and the provinces nor did it make any headway in balancing the country's tenuous relationship between religion and politics.

Religion. Politics. They are in the very air that you breathe in Pakistan. They make up the national psyche, its central nervous system. Yet they cannot be the sole means of understanding this country. I often found it disheartening to sit through class lectures, viewing slide after slide of bearded men waving guns, their eyes a cauldron of rage and hatred. It was through this volatile prism that professors discussed Pakistan in my International Affairs classes in graduate school. And it was much the same prism used by my friends and family.

The message that came across in virtually every discussion was never far from this: Pakistan is bad. Pakistan is violent. Pakistan is fearful. Pakistan is nothing but trouble. I'm not disputing the truth behind these statements. But to hear such things about one's homeland is not exactly an ego boost. The country I was born and raised in had become for the most part a social pariah. Did that mean that by extension I was too?

I finish work early today. Three small mountains of newspaper cuttings litter my desk. I've marked each article with a yellow highlighter, sifting through the rhetoric to distill facts and figures behind governance schemes. Khalid comes into the office to take away the remaining teacups. I tell him not to call me a taxi as usual. I'm in the mood to try a little experiment.

Khalid accompanies me to the gate and unlocks it. He looks nervous. I ask him if anything is wrong. He shakes his head and keeps his eyes peeled on the ground. As I get going, Khalid follows me, keeping a modest distance like a bodyguard. Maybe he thinks I don't know the way.

We are in a quiet residential neighborhood, about six blocks away from my dorm. I am modestly dressed in baggy linen pants, a knee-length jacket with a *dupatta* wrapped around my shoulders. The streets are eerily empty. A few taxis glide by with the drivers poking their heads out windows, coaxing me to climb in. Some old men sit on plastic chairs under a huge banyan tree smoking and drinking tea. They look at me in a way that says I'm breaching some sort of ban against pedestrians. It reminds me of my favorite short story by Ray Bradbury where a man gets arrested for attempting to walk the streets of Los Angeles.

By the time I reach a busy intersection, Khalid is no longer trailing behind. More taxis slow down, followed by two smirking teenage boys on Kawasaki motorcycles offering me a lift. An intrusive police officer asks me if I'm lost. Some uniformed schoolgirls break into fierce giggles. Servant women lugging baskets of produce turn in my direction with puzzled faces. A mullah with a flowing white beard urges me to cover up properly as that *dupatta* is apparently not holy enough.

I reach Aunty's home bewildered and exhausted. So much for walking home from work. The experiment is over. For good. The *chaukidar* at the gate looks perplexed and inquires about the missing taxi. I offer a weak shrug, my morale fully defeated and my *kurta* soaked in perspiration.

* * *

"You can't go there looking like that," all five of my roommates burst out in unison.

I am about to get my first fix of Pakistani mall culture at something called Jinnah Super. My roomies are taking me there on a Friday night.

"What's wrong with what I'm wearing?"

I glance down at my black yoga pants and college sweatshirt. Perfectly acceptable for a Stateside trip to the mall, but judging by the wrinkled noses and shaking heads of my inspection team, I might as well be wearing dish rags.

You are going to embarrass us all looking like a *faqir* is the overall consensus. The girls think I look like a vagrant, a bum with a begging bowl.

And who am I to argue given all that primping and preening going on before the bathroom mirrors. Eye shadows and mascara applied, hair shampooed, blow dried and fluffed out, outfits rejected and approved. Polyester is out. Linen is in. Sequins and sheer sleeves OK. *Shalwars* no. Flared pants yes. High heels a definite yes.

I change into a silky turquoise tunic that I had picked up at a clearance sale at Urban Outfitters back in Boston. My skinny white jeans meet with approval. Momina lends me a pair of dangly rhinestone earrings. She is wearing a black tank top underneath a cropped cardigan paired with her signature skin tight denims. As we step outside, she dons a snug monkey hat that matches the emerald flecks of her eyes. Oh that Momina.

I wonder if she had ever considered modeling. She would have held her ground with the best of them. Christy. Claudia. Naomi. Momina. Her name stems from the Arabic *momin*, the religious, the pure. And she tells me that she is a *Sayyed*, signifying her family's lineage to the Prophet Muhammad.

Like most all the other girls at Aunty's dorm, Momina is studying computer science. She wants to become a Software Engineer and write C++ code. Brains and beauty. She seems to have it all. We have become friendlier ever since that tussle with the waxing lady. I guess she's starting to feel sorry for me. My status has risen from that of a cobweb. Now I'm no better than an ungainly toddler learning how to walk.

The taxi drops us off at what appears to be a suburban shopping strip. There is a drugstore, a bookstore, camera shops advertising Fuji film, snack bars selling kebabs and ice cream, a hodgepodge of clothing boutiques and open air shoe stalls. An argument arises when the taxi driver demands more money than the agreed upon fare that amounted to little over a dollar. I slip him a few extra rupees that earn me the status of a softie.

"*Chalo*," Momina links her arm with mine and leads me to her favorite boutique. "Let's get you some decent clothes."

As I start pulling garments off the rack, Momina sits on a chair and smokes a cigarette. She knows the boutique owner who gives her permission to light up Marlboro menthols in her store. If she did it outside, in full view of passing strangers, mostly all male, Momina would be taken for a loose woman, maybe even a prostitute. But it is OK to be loose BCD.

BCD. Behind Closed Doors. It's an acronym I would come to learn well in Pakistan. Everything is permissible BCD if you have the means for indulgence.

Mounds of fabric drape the fitting room floor. I try on a chocolate brown pant suit. Momina nods consent and we put it in the yes pile.

"*Sunno*," she says. "I need a favor."

My head is stuck in a tight neckline and I wrestle it down.

"What did you say?"

"Listen, I, uhh, I need your help," Momina repeats and zips up the back of my top.

"*Sunno*," she whispers in my ear. "It's about my boyfriend."

"Shoot."

"We uhh, we want to go out this weekend, but you know Auntie keeps such a strict watch."

I nod sympathetically.

"But curfew is till midnight on weekends. I'm sure you can go out without any issues."

"It's not that. I, uhh, I want to be away for the whole weekend. I'm going to tell Aunty that I'm going to my parents' place in Abottabad. Promise you won't say anything."

"No prob. But what about the others?"

"They all know. But I trust them to keep their mouths shut as I trust you."

She looks worried. Gone is her cool serenity. This Momina is bound by restrictions and trying to weasel her way out BCD style. She tells me that they will go to his friend's empty apartment. He is in between moves. It will make for a discreet rendezvous.

On the way back to the dorm, Momina takes out her address book and shows me a fold up magazine cutout. It's a picture of Vaneeza and Ali. She a rising model. He an international rock star. Both are Pakistani, but they could easily pass for a glamorous South American couple, Brazilian or Venezuelan. Momina tells me they have been living together.

"Sharing love is normal," Momina declares with a sudden burst of confidence. "*Haina?*"

I nod and squeeze her arm to show my support. She smiles at me. Even the angels would be jealous.

Our taxi stops at a red light. A silver Mercedes blasting punk rock slows down on our right. Its occupants are trying to get our attention, but my roommates are stony faced and silent staring straight ahead. Momina stifles some giggles. She refuses to roll up her window. The Mercedes keeps up with us once the light turns green. Little slips of paper scribbled with phone numbers land on our laps. One hits the taxi's dashboard and sticks to the windshield. The Romeos honk and speed up. The Beauty Queen rolls her eyes. Being an absolute stunner does come with consequences, in any society.

*   *   *

Islamabad was built in the 1960's to replace Karachi as Pakistan's capital. It started out as forests of acacia trees, fields and villages nestled in the lush green vegetation surrounding the Margala Hills, the lowest range of the Himalayas. At first glance, it doesn't appear to belong to Pakistan. It is somehow too neat and insipid. But now I have come to appreciate Konstantinos Apostolos Doxiadis' grid layout that imparts a sense of order and practicality in a culture that thrives on chaos. Doxiadis. He was the Greek architect who designed this bubble in the hills. Speaking of architecture, I've become rather partial to the replicas of nuclear missiles that decorate the major traffic circles of Islamabad. They come in handy as reference points for asking directions.

Do I turn left or right at the Shaheen chowk? I often ask taxi drivers. This in turn leads into earnest lectures with the cabbie puffing on a cigarette and explaining to me that Pakistani nukes are not the death traps of some apocalyptic doomsday, they're merely symbols of nationalistic pride, a bit overkill perhaps, but nothing more than good old-fashioned pride. The lecture then veers into philosophical musings where the cabbie launches into a well rehearsed soliloquy:

Why should it only be the West who can develop nuclear technology? If we have the means and the knowledge, why shouldn't we use it? The West is just jealous. The West can't stand the thought of nukes in the hands of Muslims. We are supposed to be backward people, not modern, not progressive, let alone technologically and scientifically progressive. It's an old Western prejudice going back to the time of the Crusades. Muslims cannot be equated with modernity. We are supposed to be barbarians. So no nukes for us. But we only want them as a deterrent, for self-defense. The same reason your American government and its cronies in Israel have them.

Why should they get to keep them and we don't? Please define the meaning of a double standard.

3

NANI-MA

Rawalpindi/Mansehra, June 2003

PICTURE THIS:

A showroom SUV with leather seats, a five Disc CD changer, Dolby surround sound and an orange blossom air freshener. Gentle winding mountain road. The smell of pine needles and wood smoke. Swiss-like chalets. Fragrant herbal teas and gooey pastries. Cozy fireside chats.

Now picture this:

Tin plated buses in neon orange and green with paintings of peacocks, partridges, bears, Alpine meadows, waterfalls and Quranic verses. Roof racks piled with passengers and luggage. Chain smoking drivers yelling profanities. Horns beeping incessantly. Greasy haired urchins selling chewing gum and peanuts, Islamic leaflets, sticky syrupy drinks, and corn on the cob. Deformed beggars stretching out their hands through grimy open windows. Stray dogs, cats and goats sniffing through piles of garbage. Young men in loin cloths taking baths near open drains.

I keep shifting in my seat, trying to get more comfortable. If only I had thought of bringing a pillow for the long ride. At least I have my water bottle. But it's lodged inside my backpack which at the moment is probably functioning as someone's foot rest on the rooftop. I'm thirsty and irritable and the boy standing outside my window picking his nose and dropping its contents into a chipped saucer which contains the steaming cup of tea I had requested is not helping matters.

You've probably guessed by now which picture I'm in. You might also want to know what malevolent genie has lured me here against all free will. Actually, there is no genie involved, bad or good and though it seems highly improbable, I have voluntarily walked into this picture with my thinking apparatus fully intact. Allow me to explain why.

Three days ago, I had the choice of two weekend getaways from Islamabad. One was an invitation from a colleague at work to visit Muree, a woodsy haven, nestled in the Himalayan foothills, where I would be treated to a fancy cottage with oodles of farm fresh food and a dinner party in the works. Rumor had it that Imran Khan, the famous cricketing champ turned grass roots politician would be in attendance. Then there was another offer.

"There's a wedding in our village next Saturday," Beenish had mentioned Wednesday night. "Why don't you come along?"

And so I had decided to come along. Of course, I was expecting the journey to be somewhat outside my everyday comfort zone, which only added to its allure. Life in Islamabad was getting to be a bore. Apart from my job which consumed most of the day, there was not much to do in the evenings and weekends except for watching satellite television at the dorm and putting up with Aunty monitoring all our comings and goings as if she was running a detective agency with the boarding house as a front.

That night as I helped Beenish carry all the dirty dinner dishes to the kitchen, she told me more about the wedding. It was her second cousin whom she didn't really know all that well. But her aunts and uncles and nieces and nephews and grandparents would all be there and nothing would give them more pleasure than hosting me as their guest. *Amreekan* guest, she had added to secure my place of honor. Then she had gone on and on about the logistics of getting there. We would take a bus from Rawalpindi and then change somewhere in the Kaghan Valley for another bus to Mansehra from where we would either walk or take a rickshaw to her village.

I immediately smelled Adventure. Depending on your perspective, you could also smell Nightmare.

Pinning all my hopes on the adventure part, I packed an overnight bag at one in the morning after my roommates had gone to bed. Then I crept into the small room at the back of the house that was the servants' quarters where Beenish and her mother slept. We sat cross legged on a thin *durrie* rug and worked out the plan.

"Aunty must not know you're coming with us," Beenish warned.

I had kept it a secret from my roomies as well and told them that I was going to Lahore for the weekend to do some work related research. OK. It was a blatant lie, but I had to do it. They wouldn't have understood this hanging out with the servants business. It was a cultural taboo in Pakistan, probably a latent hangover from the Raj where the classes could not mix and there had to be a clear cut line between those who were in charge and those who were not. I had little tolerance for such nonsense.

As a child in Karachi, I was close to our servants who were treated with a great deal of affection and kindness and considered part of the family. The only glitch was the line that could not be crossed. This line was invisible and unmarked, but everyone knew where it was, everyone that is except for me. Even if I had developed the ability to see this line, I would not have wanted to stay on my side of it, which must explain why I found myself two decades later in that small cramped room with Beenish and her mother planning to sneak away with them to a family wedding. Beenish's mother was chewing on a betel leaf and eyeing me in a mixture of amusement and trepidation.

"These girls are very bad," she declared and reached for a can to spit out the red juices of her *paan*. "Why just yesterday, I caught one of them smoking in the bathroom. *Chee!*"

Beenish's mother wrinkled her nose with disgust. She wore a small silver stud on her right nostril. Her hair was streaked in various shades of orange from repeated applications of henna. She clearly liked jewelry wearing a bright assortment of glass bangles on both arms and large hoop earrings like a teenager. Her polyester floral printed *kameez* had a hole on the left armpit. I saw it when Beenish's mother reached up to slap a mosquito against the wall. She made a fresh *paan* and offered me one which I accepted. Beenish gave me an encouraging smile, glad that I was getting along with her rather domineering mother. They were so different, mother and daughter in both temperament and physique. When they talked with each other, they would sometimes switch from the Urdu that we were all conversant in to something completely different.

"*Yay kya zabaan hai?*"

I asked Beenish what language she was speaking.

"*Yay hamaree aslee zabaan hai,*" she replied. "*Hindko.*"

It was her mother tongue. Hindko. I had never heard of it before and for a moment I wondered if the word Hind might be a reference to India which used to be known during colonial times as Hindustan, the same land mass from which Pakistan was carved. Hind for Hindustan. It made sense, a fitting counterweight to the cultural amnesia racked up over years of bloodshed and conflict between India and Pakistan with both countries playing a ruthless propaganda game in brainwashing their citizens into refusing to accept their joint heritage.

I could never buy into it because my family's history was so intimately tied with India, but it pained me nonetheless that so many others had. Of course, it's hard not to get caught up in a wave of patriotism and nationalist fervor, particularly where cricket is concerned, but this crazy denial of a shared past was too much for me to handle. Why couldn't I be both Pakistani and Indian? Why did I have to choose sides? Why was all this so ridiculously complicated?

"*Hum log Hazara hain,*" Beenish added and smiled gently.

Sometimes she still looked like a little girl, no more than six or eight. It was her eyes more than any other features that were childlike filled with a sense of wonder and curiosity. They were almond shaped with the color of honey, clear and golden. Beenish had a rather flat nose and broad cheekbones. Her complexion was as fair as mine with the texture of parchment paper. Now that she had told me that she was a Hazara, I could see the Central Asian influence. I had read somewhere that Hazaras were an ethnic tribal group that traced their lineage to the Mongolian conqueror Genghis Khan. They were predominantly Shia Muslims. The majority lived in Afghanistan, where they had been persecuted by the Taliban for being infidels, mongrels, animals, the outcast Other. I hadn't realized there were also Pakistani Hazaras. It would be interesting to learn more about their way of life.

Since I had no formal clothes for the wedding, Beenish lent me her best outfits, a simple yet elegant burgundy *shalwar-kameez* in soft cotton with matching *dupatta* and a turquoise *kurta* embossed with a silver checkered pattern.

"Take these," she said. "I picked them up from the tailor yesterday. They're about your size."

Then she threw in some glass bangles and a pair of golden sandals with wedge heels.

The plan was simple enough. I would meet Beenish's mother the following morning at the small grocery store on the main road. They would get a head start so as not to be seen leaving with me. Since all this would be happening at the crack of dawn at five AM and it was nearly two in the morning, I took my leave and went back to my room to catch some sleep. But the excitement ahead kept me up and just when I was starting to doze off, there was a soft knock on the door and Beenish was standing outside asking me if I was ready. She was still in her outfit from the night before and when I asked her if she was going to change, Beenish shook her head and peeled her eyes to the floor. Aunty had refused to give her some time off.

"She needs me here," Beenish had said.

Looking at her small, sad face, I suspected that it was not just Aunty who had bullied her into staying, but her mother as well, who hadn't relished the thought of cooking, cleaning and doing the dishes while being ordered about by a bunch of "ungrateful girls" as she referred to my roommates. Let her daughter take over the duties at the dorm. One more weekend wouldn't make much of a difference.

I was crushed that Beenish would not be accompanying us.

"Don't worry," she had said. "You'll have fun."

By the time, I was safely out the door, I half ran to the grocery store since it was almost sunrise and I was afraid that Beenish's mother had already left without me. But there she was waiting, sitting on a rickety staircase and munching on some *roti*. She tore off a piece and offered it to me, but I had already eaten one of my fig and date energy bars on the way. They had been in my suitcase all this time and it was a moment of pure exhilaration when I found them tucked away in a zippered compartment, the package a bit squashed but otherwise just the same as when I had first seen it on a Whole Foods shelf in Boston just over three months ago.

"*Chalo*," Beenish's mother stood up and threw a small cloth bundle over her shoulder.

"Zeeshan!" she hollered and a small boned boy joined us from across the street. He was carrying a plastic bag filled with bananas. Whatever happens on the journey, at least we won't be going hungry I thought, glad that I had brought the entire box of energy bars.

"My son," Beenish's mother said and nudged the boy's shoulder in my direction.

We solemnly shook hands. He looked about twelve or thirteen. I noticed that one of his eyeballs did not move as though it were made of glass. We walked along the edge of the road and hailed a taxi in the direction of Rawalpindi.

*   *   *

In its essence, *Pir Wadhai* has the same energy level as Grand Central Station. But let's not kid ourselves. Rawalpindi's commuting hub certainly does not look like the real thing. There are no polished marble floors, no helpful information booth, no printed timetables, no cash machines, no snack bars, no comfortable benches, no grand imposing clock, and no busy commuters dashing about with wheeled bags, tote bags, messenger bags, laptop bags and all manner of handsome purses, attaché cases and briefcases. Of course, there are commuters at *Pir Wadhai*, but not of the kind you would see in New York City.

The commuters of *Pir Wadhai* are a hearty cross station of Pakistani society. There are old men in beards and skull caps. There are husbands and fathers in flowing *shalwar-kameez* and sturdy fisherman style sandals. A few are clean shaven. Others have close cropped goatees and shapely sideburns. There are high school boys in baseball caps and jeans and T-shirts that read Adidas, Nike, Reebok.

"Change dollars?" they inquire as I step out of the taxi.

There are sturdy faced mothers with babies and toddlers. There are toothless grandmothers mumbling on prayer beads. There are young college age girls like my roommates. Some of them are pretty, their hair in braids tied up with ribbons, their clothes a riot of colors and patterns, so when they move collectively, it's almost as if I'm watching a train of butterflies. Sometimes, they turn and stare at me and cover their mouths to stifle their giggles.

I walk alongside all these people, following Beenish's mother and Zeeshan who are leading the way. Together, we wade through the human tide of *Pir Wadhai*.

"*Jaldi, jaldi*," Beenish's mother urges me to hurry along. We make our way towards a waiting minivan. No one is inside it except for the driver. He pats the empty seat beside him and curls a finger in my direction. I turn around to look for my travel mates and see Zeeshan buying some oranges from a greasy haired urchin. His mother shoves me forward and I nearly fall face down on the front seat which is where all foreigners sit or so I'm told. I have some issues with the foreigner bit and I can't understand why the back of the van is off limits and I'm already worrying about the smug smiles and sidelong glances coming from the driver, but it's all too much to deal with so early in the morning. The van is starting to fill up with more passengers. Men and women file into separate rows so the seating code is gender specific. It doesn't seem to apply to the front row.

The driver lights a fresh cigarette and slowly reverses, his hand sliding down ever so casually and resting on my thigh. I nudge Zeeshan who is beside me by the window seat and we trade places with the boy in the middle as a buffer against the randy driver. I can't see or talk with Zeeshan's mother who is sitting three rows behind us with a group of mothers and fresh faced young girls. The driver gives one last impatient honk. A teenage boy acting as our conductor stands on the edge of the van's open door and shouts our destination.

"Mansehra! Mansehra!"

When no further passengers come forth, the boy slides the door shut and perches on the gear box.

*   *   *

They enjoy looking at me, shyly at first, wrapping their *dupattas* over their mouth to cover the all too obvious smiles. They whisper amongst each other and stare with dark bold inquisitive eyes, whisper and stare. Some of them run around me in circles, giggling and pointing. I should like to think it's because of the excitement of a stranger in their midst, but I can't be entirely sure that all this scrutiny is purely harmless. At some level, I feel judged by these girls, made to feel like the class idiot in front of a savvy group of eighth graders. It doesn't matter that I'm wearing Beenish's turquoise *kurta* with my white cotton *shalwar*, a maroon shawl loosely draped over my head and shoulders. They may have a sister or friend named Maliha, but something about me betrays me as *ajnabee*, a foreigner. Perhaps it's my facial expression, just a tad too eager and curious or maybe the cut of the *kurta* is all wrong and I'm one of those fashion victims whose embarrassing photos appear in the back pages of glossy women's magazines.

"Jeetay raho, jeetay raho!"

An old woman with stringy white hair and chocolate brown skin thick with wrinkles shuffles in our direction and sits next to me on the charpoy. Beenish's mother addresses her as Ammi-jan, an endearment for mother. I can tell right away that both mother and daughter have the same spunky spirit only there seems to be more kindness and compassion in the matriarch whose toothless smile uplifts my mood as do her words. Long may you live!

Tea arrives on a round stainless steel tray big as a cartwheel. It is so hot that I pour some in a saucer to cool it off and take small sips. *Nani-ma* as I've christened Beenish's grandma notices my gesture and does the same. We are joined by three young women, two of her other daughters and a daughter in-law. They look cheerful and pleasant and one of them reminds me of my aunt in India, with her aquiline nose and kohl embellished eyes. She offers me a plate of Marie biscuits. We all look at each other and smile in that way strangers do to make themselves feel more comfortable in uncertain surroundings. I stretch out my sore legs and yearn for a nap.

The six hour journey by public transport had gone surprisingly well, almost too well considering the chaotic send off from Rawalpindi. We had lunch at a small village in the Kaghan valley and feasted on *chapli* kebabs rolled up in fresh baked *naan*. Zeeshan looked after me as though I was his own sister, buying my mineral water at rest stops, keeping the driver's paws at a safe distance. When we stopped to transfer to a different vehicle and had to walk a few hundred yards, he told me to cover not just my head with my shawl, but also my face. I saw how the other women were clutching a fistful of fabric over their mouth and nose and tried to copy them, but I couldn't get the hang of it. My shawl was not large enough and it kept slipping and I found it hard to keep myself veiled in this manner and walk fast at the same time.

Beenish's mother was clearly an expert. She had shielded her face in a layer of her floral printed chador and somehow tucked its end behind her ears so she could be hands free. It was odd to see her like this, odd not to be able to make out her fleshy lips and *paan* stained teeth. The costume she wore in public was an armor of dignity and protection which is one function of the Muslim veil. By hiding the woman's adornments, it gives her license to be visible in the public domain, to see without being seen. But I still couldn't get the point of it.

Irrespective of my covered head and partially covered face, I knew that I was still being looked at, ogled by dozens upon dozens of male eyes in those dusty crowded streets just outside of Mansehra. It was a nuisance to deal with this while being all wrapped up like a mummy. But it was the custom and I had to abide by it and not doing so would have only made me stand out even more and earn the wrath of conservative minded denizens in this rural heartland where customs and culture were mostly allegiance to tribal norms, rather than Islam or what may be regarded as "Pakistani".

"Aao, beti, aao."

Nani-ma's voice breaks my train of thoughts. They're bringing dinner now, more cartwheel platters with bowls of curry and *daal,* heaping mounds of rice and oblong slabs of fresh hot *naan* seared with black charcoal marks. There is one vegetable curry that suits me just fine. A spicy *aloo gobi,* potatoes with cauliflower. I mix it on my plate with some rice and *daal* and eat with my fingers like everyone else. Nani-ma is watching me, her wizened old eyes as sharp as a blackbird's.

I am touched by her simplicity and friendliness, the very antithesis of Aunty's formal treatment back in Islamabad. Now just a hundred and fifty kilometers outside the city in a Pakistani village, whose name I don't even know, with people who are absolute strangers to me, I feel so much more at home.

"Chalyay, chalyay, oopur chalyay!"

One of the eighth grade members of the staring mafia is tugging at the sleeve of my *kurta* urging me to come upstairs for some stargazing. I steel a quick glance at Nani-ma who is licking her fingers clean having polished off every grain of rice from her plate. She seems too preoccupied to look my way and soon I am surrounded by an entire gang of children who won't take no for an answer. I put aside my half finished dinner and follow my escorts to a stony staircase on the corner of the open courtyard. It's next to a faucet with a small drain built into the cement floor that functions as a sink where the daughter-in-law is squatting on her haunches and doing the dishes.

I ought to be helping her with the chore, but I know that she would see it as an insult, much the same way my small offerings of fruit and cakes were politely ignored in the Middle Eastern households where I was invited for lunch or dinner. We can provide for ourselves and for you, just fine, thanks but no thanks was the unspoken text.

It was the one constant in all my travels around the world. The most generous people were the ones who had the least in material possessions. And it was in the smaller towns, rather than the cities, where my status as a stranger/foreigner/outsider was not a source of discomfort, but something to embrace, even enjoy.

*   *   *

The following morning, I wake up to a panoramic view. All around me as far as the eye can see are fields of wheat unfurling like a giant tapestry in shades of ochre, gold and rust. The star studded sky has given way to a soft translucent blue pasted with feathery clouds. I am all alone on the rooftop where I had slept on a rope bed in the cool night air alongside the children and women of the household, Nani-ma, her daughter-in-law, and her three daughters, including Beenish's mother. By a stroke of luck, there had been a light meteor shower which delighted the kids. We had a slumber party, Mansehra style telling each other folk tales of evil *jinns* and clever viziers, sad princes and village idiots.

I had recited a Pakistani childhood fable about an impoverished fisherman's wife who is not satisfied with any of the fairy mermaid's wishes given to her husband. In the end, she goes too far by asking for the ultimate wish, to become God, and the distraught fisherman begs the mermaid to take away all their riches and return them to their mud brick hut where they were poor but happy. Everyone clapped as I finished the story and there was unanimous consensus that the fisherman's wife had been blinded by greed and power and deserved to be put back in her proper place. Nani-ma sung an old Afghan folk song.

Ba yaad dari, she chorused. *Ba yaad dari.*

When I asked her what the lyrics meant, she said they were about the memory of good old days. And then she gave me her toothless smile, turned on her side and was soon snoring gently.

How I admire Nani-ma's strength and sense of self. She doesn't seem to question her existence so much as simply live it. And then I see her out in the fields, a white haired, hunchbacked goblin scything the wheat with a machete. She looks healthy and strong, so purposeful in her physical labor that is impervious of age or gender or any other hindrance to her subsistence as a farmer.

Downstairs, the walls of the courtyard are lined with bushels of fresh cut wheat. Beenish's mother is nowhere in sight, but one of the daughters ushers me into a noisy room full of women and children. Their faces are all new and I am told they are the groom's side of the family. It is Nani-ma's youngest daughter's daughter who is getting married. The *nikkah* or the religious ceremony that formally concedes the couple as man and wife has already taken place in the groom's village. There will be a party tonight, a reception of sorts, to celebrate the wedding at the house of the groom's aunt who lives nearby.

"*Bohot maza aaye gah!*" It's going to be a blast!

One of the women declares and pokes the knee of the middle aged lady sitting beside her. They giggle like silly school girls. Daughter-in-law brings me a breakfast tray of homemade yogurt with chapatti and a mug of steaming chai. To my utter horror, she has also thrown in a few strips of torn up cotton from discarded clothing on the tray as though they are nothing more than paper napkins with which to wipe my mouth. Of course, they don't escape the gaze of the stareathon committee watching my every move with rapt attention and now they are nudging each other and exchanging whispers and

soon the entire room knows that it's my time of the month and I'm
burning with embarrassment.

"Hullo. Very happy to meet you. My name is Seema."

A young woman with coal black eyes and shiny black hair
braided down her back introduces herself and sits next to me. She
looks no more than sixteen or eighteen. When she smiles her eyes
remain sad as though they are incapable of registering the emotion
of her upturned mouth.

"You are coming from America, yes?" Seema asks.

"I live in America," I reply. "But I'm from Pakistan. From Karachi."

"Karachi," she says with a sigh. "I have been there one time. To visit
my brother. It is too big city. I feel so lost there. I tell my brother to take
me to the sea. So he take me one day to Clifton beach. Very big waves! I
love it so much. I spend all day looking at waves. It is very nice."

"I grew up near Clifton beach."

We look at each other and smile. I am taken aback with her eyes.
They are so very sad. What could it be? I gently broach the topic in
Urdu.

"Tumhareen aankho mai itna afsos kyoon hai?"

"Ji," Seema replies and looks down at her hands. "Ji..."

I feel as though she wants to tell me more, to give voice to her
inner pain and sorrow and slowly the words pour out and I learn
about the loss of her mother who died in a car accident when Seema
was just a little girl. My eyes well up with tears and I offer her my
condolences which sound empty and hollow as they often sound to
those who are still grieving.

"Kya malum. Kismet ki baat hain."

Seema attempts to brush off what she has just revealed by casting it
off to the whims of fate. What is written is written. We must accept
and move on with our lives.

"Sahee kai rahee ho."

I tell her she's saying the right thing. At the same time, I wonder
privately if I really believe Seema's fatalistic doctrine.

Our sober discussion is interrupted by the sound of loud
Bollywood music. Someone has brought a Sony boom box into the
room and popped in a cassette with the familiar lyrics from the mega
hit Dilse. A group of girls start dancing in the middle of the room to
Shahrukh Khan's famous Chaiyya Chaiyya number. In the movie he is

singing and gyrating on top of a moving train with a gorgeous village seductress as they travel through the lush green countryside.

"*Chaiyya Chaiyya Chaiyya Chaiyya*!!"

The girls sing aloud the chorus in discordant voices, their bodies moving in perfect measure to the pounding beat.

Some of the older women clap and ululate with their tongues. One of them stands up and grooves with the music, her heavy hips swaying with expert ease. The song ends and now we hear the familiar strains of *Ae Ajnabee*, one of my all time favorites. It's much slower, the lyrics heavy with melancholy and longing. Something comes over me, a nameless feeling that makes me throw aside all sense of propriety and shyness.

I tie my *dupatta* around the waist like a sash and make my way into the dancing circle. The girls make room and start copying my movements. I shuffle my feet side to side salsa style. I twirl my hands like a flamenco dancer. Some of the girls stand aside to watch and then one by one, the group disbands. Feeling the full weight of the music, I begin to turn counterclockwise, spinning in slow circles with my eyes closed. When the song ends, there is a burst of applause and the doorway is crammed with women and children. They are all grinning madly.

* * *

"*Shabash bachi shabash!*"

Nani-ma offers praise. I hadn't realized she has been part of the audience witnessing my display of pure craziness. Now I've had it. Word will soon spread that the unassuming house guest from *Amreeka* is pure entertainment. Indeed it does. The rest of the day, while waiting for the wedding festivities to begin, I go from house to house, visiting curious neighbors who cannot wait to see the nutty foreigner in action. I enjoy it for a while--make that a very short while--and then it gets out of control.

By the fifth house call, it is clear they have turned me into their very own Energizer bunny. It's getting rather tiresome. So I quit and attempt to walk back to Nani-ma's house by myself. Attempt is the key word. A girl runs up behind me and grabs my arm.

"Where do you think you're going?"

"*Nani-ma kay ghar.*"

"You can't just wander off like that. Are you daft or something?"

"What's your problem?"

"What's yours?"

We stare daggers at each other and then she bursts out laughing.

"Oh dear. I'm so sorry. That was pretty bad manners. I, uhh, I just didn't want you to get lost. You're the American, aren't you? I heard Aunty say you were coming from Boston. I have heard of it. From my teacher in school. It is close to New York. Yankee stadium and Rainbow Room. You have been there?"

"Sort of."

"Wow!"

"Can we go back to the house? I need the bathroom."

"Yes, yes, let us go back. This way!"

So we head back to the house I was trying to flee from five minutes ago and to my utter amazement we are all alone. The lady who had sequestered me in her living room with a ghetto blaster and Bollywood music a half hour ago and asked, no, commanded me to dance, has mysteriously disappeared. Thank heavens.

Shabnam's English is excellent. She attended a convent for her primary school education and now she's enrolled at Hazara University in Mansehra where she is doing a course in chartered accountancy. Her dream is to own a beauty salon and offer the best bridal makeup in town. Shabnam talks about a place called Rose Beauty Parlor in Mehar where one of her friends works. They specialize in skin bleaching, but that's old school, according to Shabnam. She wants to do custom eyebrow settings and European style haircuts.

When I ask Shabnam if she is Hazara, she nods with pride. I am confused. The National Geographic article I had read about Hazaras in Afghanistan portrayed a very different scenario. Some of the Afghan Hazaras were ashamed of their ethnicity. They went as far as keeping it a secret, given the history of persecution against them from various regimes among which the Taliban were the most brutish. When I mention this to Shabnam, she nods again and tells me that she has a cousin from Afghanistan, Shafiq, a school teacher who was living there in 2001 when the Taliban engineered a massacre of young Hazara men on a cold winter morning.

"They rounded them up like dogs and sheep and shot them in public."

"But why?"

"Because they were Shia. That's all."

"How awful. But what about your cousin?"

"He was in another village at the time. Near Bamian. The Taliban had set fire to the bazaar. My cousin had to hide in a cave."

"Did they find him?"

"Eventually."

Shabnam shakes her head with sorrow. But she is still glad to be a Hazara. It's what makes her different from others and it even gives her role models like Saira Baitool, the first Hazara woman to pilot a jet in the Pakistani air force.

Now it's my turn to be impressed. I envy Shabnam's poise. Like Nani-ma, she is grounded in her own skin and not afraid to show it. I wish I could be more like these women and do away with all my insecurities. In a way, I feel a certain affinity with the Hazaras. We are at some level the perennial outsiders in our own country.

"*Chalo*," Shabnam says as she rises and extends her hand to help me up. "We're going to be late for the wedding party."

"Will you come with me to Nani-ma's?" I ask.

"Who??"

"Nani…oh never mind. Just come with me next door. I have to change my clothes."

"As you wish."

No one is there, but in the daughter-in-law's bedroom where my bags are kept, Beenish's burgundy *shalwar-kameez* has been freshly ironed and neatly placed on the bed along with her sandals and bangles. How I miss her.

* * *

The courtyard opens towards a makeshift patio with an awning secured by wooden rods and a thick blanket. Hazy sunlight mingles with wisps of smoke. I smell clove cigarettes and sweet tobacco.

Shabnam nudges me in the direction of some shallow stone steps. We enter a large rectangular room where a party is in full swing.

Young girls are sitting on rough tribal rugs draped across the earthenware floor. Someone is playing the *dholak*. There is the metallic sound of a spoon beating against the drum. A chorus of tinny voices rises in crescendo presumably singing wedding songs in Hindko or Pashto or Dari. They clap their hands to the beat as they sing. Groups of older ladies huddle on beds pushed back against two walls. A mother breast feeds her child and taps her knees. All the women have kohl rimmed eyes and a pageantry of color adorns their dresses. My outfit goes down well. Someone calls me a *dulan* or bride. I meet the real *dulan* who kisses me warmly on both cheeks. It is foolhardy to even think of blending in. All eyes are on me, the stranger who somehow looks so familiar. The singing halts abruptly. The *dholak* player appears to have one hand frozen in mid air as her ferocious drumming halts. A hushed silence gives way to murmurs and then a request.

Will you dance for us?

4

THE STORY TELLER'S BAZAAR

Islamabad/Peshawar, June 2003

PESHAWAR??

As soon as I utter the word, grim assessments and warnings flood my ears, from well meaning advice givers.

"You won't come back alive!" asserts Momina.

"Says who?"

"Says me, your guide on the do's and don'ts of Pakistani culture."

"Thank you guide. I believe I can handle this one on my own."

"You'll come to regret it. You won't make it back in one piece."

"Yes, I think you said that already. Anything else to add before I whack you on the head for being a total nincompoop?"

The Beauty Queen simply shrugs her shoulders and applies some lip gloss.

She's not just my roommate anymore, but a friend and confidante. For nearly two months, we have been conducting our lives in close proximity, sharing the same bedroom and bathroom, eating breakfast together every morning, dinner on most nights. Though I know all this is temporary, there comes a point in travel when even the most fleeting of situations become a cherished constant, the only known reality.

"I'm glad you're staying on," says Momina.

"Me too."

"But you're still nuts."

"I know."

"And I love you just the same, you little nincompoopoo!"

Momina tosses a pillow in my face and picks up her ringing mobile. I step out on the balcony with my guidebook, but my mind keeps racing and I can't concentrate on the highlighted paragraphs and all the miniscule notes scribbled in the margins. Maybe Momina was right. It was a bit crazy to run off with the servants for the weekend. I didn't think anyone would find out about Mansehra. I had kept it quiet and just went about my business staying busy with work and copious amounts of reading late into the night. Then a few days after we were back, Beenish's mother had said something idiotic along the lines of how well I had danced at the wedding and she said this in front of Aunty who wasted no time in employing her sleuthing powers to assemble the missing pieces. I was convinced that I was going to get thrown out.

"In the future, I expect you to tell me where you're going, with whom and when you're coming back. Is that clear?"

"Yes, Aunty."

"This is a good, clean, respectable place. I don't want you to become a bad influence on the girls with all your American freedoms. Is that clear?"

"Yes, Aunty."

"If you're going to stay here, you must respect our ways and control your behavior. Am I making myself clear?"

"Yes, Aunty."

It could have been far worse. I took the scolding in stride visualizing Aunty as a Victorian headmistress in a corseted frock and feathered hat. And then I thought of stealing the *paan* that Beenish's mother kept in her room in a round stainless steel box. Just to teach her a lesson. Oh never mind. I should have known that woman was no good at keeping her mouth shut. All she was good for was chewing *paan* and bossing around her hapless daughter.

Beenish was so excited to have me back. "See, I told you it would be fun!" she had exclaimed and given me a warm hug.

I returned her clothes and jewelry minus the shoes which I had lost the night of the wedding party, a most exuberant and joyful affair of song and dance, the likes of which I shall probably never see again.

But now what? My research is nearly finished and I have not been assigned any new projects at work. I could try looking for another job, another unpaid internship in Islamabad's vast sector of NGO's and policy institutes. It would give me stability and the comfort of a routine. I could go on living in Islamabad not just as a traveler, but as a resident who has a landlady and a consortium of boisterous roommates. Stable, but boring.

I keep thinking about Nani-ma and her fields of wheat, the humble village where an entire clan of strangers had made me feel at home, the green hills of Mansehra, the buzz of Rawalpindi and Pir Wadhai, the randy bus driver, the commotion on the bus, the bumpy bus ride. I need to feel that energy again. I need to keep on traveling. Cut loose from this bubble in the hills and see the real Pakistan. My first stop will be Peshawar.

Peshawar??

*   *   *

It's asking for trouble...You haven't exactly picked a good time... The MMA just passed the Shariat bill...Those bearded chaps are tearing up Bollywood posters ... You'd better drape yourself in a tent.

Fear. Mistrust. Paranoia. That's the consensus when it comes to NWFP, Pakistan's North West Frontier province, the country's poster child of religious fervor and lawlessness with all manners of barriers and restrictions given the recent Islamist victory. Definitely no place for a single young girl, certainly out of bounds if she has no official plans or VIP status, major fiasco if she is totally ignorant about the local customs and newly arrived in the country as an American citizen.

Oh Dear.

It's not just my desire to go to Peshawar that meets with disapproval at the office. It's the very thought of traveling solo in Pakistan as a woman. Whoever heard of such a thing? It's simply

not done. I might as well be wearing a sign emblazoned in bold
black letters.

DISASTER ON BOARD!

So why am I willing to upend societal norms and risk my life on the
open road in a country with zero tolerance for lone female vagabonds
when I have the option of staying put in an air conditioned office in
Islamabad, checking email and sipping cupfuls of tea and doing
nothing more physically taxing than photocopying the latest policy
report by Human Rights Watch.

I have a long answer and a short one. Let me start with the shorter.
Peshawar.

It gets more hopeful when one of my colleagues labels me an
Eccentric. I am encouraged to be one with the masses and take cheap
public transportation, and above all, to ride on top of all the buses
for the best views.

The following Friday evening after work, I grab a small duffle
bag from underneath my desk, lock up the office, and flag a taxi to
the Daewoo bus station in Rawalpindi, just in time for the 6:15
service to Peshawar.

Anwar will be waiting for me when I arrive. We have stayed in
touch since the Khyber Pass trip. That's all the support I need, but
even without Anwar, I would have come to Peshawar anyhow, fully
aware of the risks and fully determined not to cave in. I am used to
traveling this way.

In my travels throughout Egypt, Jordan, Lebanon, Syria and
Turkey, I constantly skirted the line between adventure and stupidity,
plunging headlong into disastrous situations when my desire to live
in the moment and be utterly spontaneous outweighed the obvious
dangers. Trusting strangers in strange lands became my motto. And
even when that trust was betrayed, I would still remain unguarded
and open to the next wayward turn in a journey that had no agenda
or itinerary. I had embarked upon that journey because I needed to
know at the age of twenty eight what else I was capable of achieving
beyond the bullet points of my resume. The journey had to be
difficult. This was precisely why I had chosen to backpack solo for
an entire year in the Middle East. The expedition pushed my limits
and because I was younger with a devil may care attitude I did not

sense any fear and even when I did, I was able to overcome it and move on. I traveled for the sake of movement alone.

I am not so sure I would behave in that same rash manner in Pakistan, which ought to be more comfortable turf than the Mideast, but strangely enough it's not. Part of the problem is logistics and by now it's clear to me that Islamabad's infrastructure, unlike Cairo, Amman, Beirut, Damascus and Istanbul, is not designed to be user friendly to the independent adventurer. There is no subway, no decent bus service. My experience with Islamabad's taxi drivers has been spotty at best, ranging from open propositions from the horny ones to raging monologues from the politically disenfranchised.

As for walking, I had already discovered that it was a futile endeavor unless you really wanted to turn yourself into a public spectacle. Without a car at your disposal, preferably with your own chauffeur or friends who had cars and were willing to take you around town, there seemed to be no other way to move about. Besides, Islamabad did not entice me as a city worth exploring. It was the nation's capital and rather stodgy and lifeless. If I had come to Pakistan to unearth some culture, I certainly wasn't going to find it here. I had to go somewhere far more colorful and hazardous.

According to the press, both local and international, Peshawar was becoming the heartland of the Taliban and religious extremists. Guns were as easy to buy as produce at a farmer's market. Smugglers were rampant dealing with everything from drugs to appliances. Women had to cover up from head to toe.

Maybe my colleagues were right. I was just asking for trouble. There was only one way to find out.

* * *

"Welcome to Peshawar!"

Anwar acknowledges me with a smile and a handshake. We have met like this before at the Daewoo bus station. Last time I was in town, he had whisked me off on a treacherous mountain pass towards the Afghan border. But now I'm longing to stay put. In Peshawar.

"New car?"

Anwar grins and taps the hood of his sparkling new Pajero. We head towards his house where I will be staying for the weekend. It's a small bungalow, modestly decorated and unusually quiet by Pakistani standards.

"After you, Madame!"

Anwar holds the door open and props himself on a daybed next to his wife Salma who has a plate of oranges resting on her lap. She picks up the fruit and Anwar steals it from her hand. This just prompts her to feed him more oranges. One by one, she puts them in his mouth and he beams with pleasure. Feeling as though I'm intruding on a rather private moment, I fix my attention on the large flat screen TV depicting the news with the volume on mute. Anwar's baby daughter is napping nearby in a bassinet. She has a thick mop of black hair and skin that is paler than both her parents.

Salma has a cherubic moon like face with thin sculpted eyebrows and smoldering black eyes. I smile at her, not quite knowing what to say. Salma had been rather distant and standoffish during my last visit. It was understandable. I was gallivanting around town with her husband in tow. Of course she didn't like me. But now she comes up and kisses me warmly on the cheeks. I complement her *kurta*. Salma tells me it's from Multan, her hometown, which is famous for its *karhai*, hand crafted embroidery. Soon we are huddled in her bedroom like a couple of teenagers mad about clothes. Salma opens a huge wooden armoire that takes up an entire wall and pulls out hanger after hanger of *kurtas* in palettes of turquoise, vermillion, violet, mustard yellow and parrot green. She continues the fashion show by showing me her collection of Kashmiri shawls and insists on lending me a *chador* for my wanderings about town.

When I ask her to accompany me for a shopping spree in the bazaar the following morning, Salma shakes her head in fierce protest as though I had asked her to hang out at a slaughter house. Her tailor still pays house calls with bolts of cloth and jewelry just like they used to in the old days. I'm starting to get the feeling that what comprises adventure to me is to Salma as to countless other Pakistani women, nothing but one massive pain in the neck. Who would want to go out in this heat and dust, wandering around in the filthy streets, only to be ogled and harassed by perverts and beggars? Only mad foreigners and other lost souls.

They float around in lightweight pastel colored shawls or a large *dupatta* draped around their heads and upper bodies. Contrary to what I had heard, the majority of women in the streets of Peshawar are not shielded in tent-like *burqas*. I have definitely gone overboard donning a tight maroon headscarf and a woolen beige shawl on a sweltering day with the mercury hitting forty-five degrees Celsius. My thin cotton *kameez* is drenched in sweat and I wear my large shawl toga style to avoid tripping over its ends. Despite the cumbersome layers of clothing, the maddening heat and the complete foreignness of my surroundings, excitement courses through my veins as I start exploring the narrow alleys of the old storyteller's bazaar known as *Kisakahani*. The name celebrates memories of traders and travelers who would cross over mountains from Kabul, Kashgar and Samarkand and converge in Peshawar to swap their tales.

Being Sunday, most of the shops are closed and my presence elicits more curiosity. Young men chuckle at the sight of a solitary girl snapping pictures of ancient decaying buildings and rickety doors. A flock of children trails me from a distance. I spin around and go shutter mad. The attention I receive is not hostile and the most refreshing aspect of it is the way people handle their natural inquisitiveness about seeing a stranger in their midst. They simply come up to me and ask who I am and where I come from. Sometimes, they question me in Pashto and are surprised when I can't answer back. The camera is a dead giveaway of my outsider status. Instead of driving a wedge, it helps break the ice.

It is not long before I find a local guide. A bony little boy in dusty flip flops and a snow-white skull cap leads me by hand around the neighborhood. He instantly picks up on my fondness for rotting old houses and takes me to some real gems. Nowadays, they serve as tiny ateliers for tailors, bookbinders and weavers, often cramming a family of ten in one room. The utility principle is more important than preserving the intricate wooden carvings, fading arabesque paintings and imagined opulence of a bygone era.

"Now I show you Dilip Kumar's house," announces my guide, referring to the famous Indian actor who at one time had lived in

Peshawar's old *havelis*. I follow along, enjoying the simple friendliness so easily encountered just by virtue of being out and about. Every time we pass shopkeepers sitting inside half shuttered shops, eating lunch or sharing a cup of tea with friends, they turn their heads and look towards me with interest, slightly puzzled at my hard to place looks. There is none of the harassment that my knowledgeable well wishers had warned me about.

I appreciate the subtle acknowledgement I receive from the men, from a courteous nod to a warm *salaam*. Often, I detect a hint of admiration, even a gleam of adventure in the male eyes that scan my every move and gesture. This is quite unlike my experience in Islamabad where men either pretend that women don't exist or go all hormonal every time they encounter the female species. Here in the old city of Peshawar, I feel like a person instead of an object, my dignity restored and respected by an ancient code of conduct that is far more civilized.

I stop for a drink at a small juice stall and order a salty *lassi*. A boy wearing a black Nike baseball cap nods a polite welcome. I meet the owner's son who speaks fluent English with a twangy American accent. He tells me has spent ten years in America, where he went on scholarship to the University of Nebraska. I blink back surprise and glance at his seventy something father dicing fresh oranges. He bombards me with a string of questions in patchy English that he has no doubt picked up from his dashing young son.

How much is salary for doctor in America? What about salary for teacher and car sales man? How much is car? How much is banana and coconut? How much is juice bar? How much is juice?

The old man registers my responses with calculations on a chalkboard.

"I go Amreeka! I make good life!"

His son laughs as if what he has just heard is really not that funny.

The father leans forward and motions me to come closer to the counter. His amber eyes scan my face slowly, deliberately. He nods and smiles, murmurs something in Pashto, then nods his head and smiles again. I tug at my headscarf, hike up the ends of my chador. The man stoops and pulls out a carved wooden box, rummages inside it and snaps the lid closed. His fingers curl open to reveal a lapis lazuli pendant. I accept it as a gift. We say goodbye in the traditional way, right hands placed above the heart. The handsome son gives me a flirtatious wink.

Back into the streets, I head towards a music store. The smiling young attendant plays samples of Pashtun music on a boom box. He opens a glass cabinet and picks out more cassettes. As soon as the music starts up, teenage boys filter into the store, gleefully gaping at the odd sight of a chador-clad girl drumming her fingers to the sound of the *rabab*. An appreciative male audience gathers around me and competes with another on their suggestions on what I should buy. Someone jokes about the Taliban.

He: *They're just a bunch of hooligans out on a power trip. Why does the West take them so seriously?*

Me: *Those so called hooligans have stirred a lot of trouble. They must be held accountable.*

He: *Accountable? By who, may I ask? By me, you, or your benevolent American government??*

I change tacks and ask if there is a ban on music in Peshawar as pointed out by my pals in Islamabad. Everyone hoots with laugher. Heads shake vigorously from side to side. I walk out with a dozen new tapes for my walkman.

5

FROM BURQAS TO CATWALKS

Karachi, July 2003

NATASCHA ATLAS SPINS WITH ZZ TOP and Pink Floyd followed by the latest Bollywood and Bhangra. The dance floor pulses with hormones. Girls in halter-tops and tight flared denims shimmy and sway, rake fingers through curtains of jet-black tresses. Blue strobe lights freeze frame their moves like time-lapse photography. Guys high on Ecstasy cluster in a dancing circle, raising their arms shoulder high, hands weaving elaborate arcs, legs lunging and bending and squatting like a stoner's version of Tai-Chi.

Smoke rises from hookahs and joints. Couples smooch. Someone asks for another bottle of Johnny Walker Black label. The host of the party doubles as a bartender. He looks like an early 1980's version of Rob Lowe with his sea green eyes and chiseled jaw line. His parents are abroad and he has taken the liberty of throwing a little bash at their seaside bungalow. The guests are the hippest and naughtiest people in town.

For the umpteenth time, I readjust my glasses and resist the urge to fold my arms and stroke a troubled chin. The rational part of my brain veers into serious psychoanalysis.

Ahem. Such wanton displays of hedonism are quite typical among the idle elite caught up in the trappings of aimless pursuits ...

Then my emotional side takes over, hammering the heart like a woodpecker gone nuts.

Would you get a load of this!

I ask my friend Imran who has accompanied me to the party to pinch my forearm. It hurts. So this must be real. Or maybe not. I ask him to do it again. Ouch! I cannot be dreaming. Impossible. Highly unfathomable.

If this really were a dream, than that gorgeous bartending host would make a bee line in my direction instead of chatting up some girl who would give Madonna a major inferiority complex. Of course this is for real. Never mind the fact that someone is playing Twister with my memory. Imran brings me a vodka tonic despite my repeated requests for mineral water. We soak up the atmosphere melding onto the packed dance floor until the wee hours of the morning.

The ceiling fan in my room dangles from a long stem, its dusty blades revolving in a lazy swirl, unable to move the stale air. My arms and face are damp with sweat and I lie in bed trying to remember where I am and for how long I have been asleep. It feels as though there is a truckload of cement on top of my head. It hurts if I sit up so I remain on my back watching the fan go round and round. My eyes stay focused on the spinning fan. I find its repetitive motion soothing. And maybe because it's late and I'm still groggy and disoriented and limp from the heat, that I start to see the fan's journey and mine as one and the same. We are going nowhere.

Four days have passed since I've been back in Karachi, but already it has thrown me completely off kilter. There is so much to absorb, so much to learn that some days I'm not sure if I can cope with the newness of my surroundings. It is not the newness of climate or food or language, but the newness of being in a place that feels so familiar and foreign at the same time.

I cannot stop thinking about that party. A seaside rave. A chance invitation from a friend of a friend of a friend. I had never been to a rave before. It was the last thing I was expecting in Karachi of all places. I'm up for anything now. Something tells me that Karachi is not going to disappoint. It is my home after all and I love it to pieces. Don't I, don't I?

* * *

"We got gobs of foreign aid from the Americans because we struck a deal to nab the fundos, Pakistanis abroad are transferring their assets to local banks and Musharraf is Mr. Level Headed in Washington think tanks," Nadir declares.

It's our standard dinner conversation hovering around politics. Tonight, my cousin is trying to convince me that 9/11 has been a major boost to Pakistan. I'm not sure if I buy into Nadir's reasoning. Siding with the war against terror, a war that you did not create, but one which you must fight, appeasing your countrymen as well as the country that wants them dead, is not a win-win situation. Something has to give and that something has been Pakistan's standing as the terror den of the world with a litany of setbacks to overcome. In Karachi, there is much talk in the news about all the random killings. According to the daily headlines, people are being murdered like flies. There appears to be not a shred of morality left.

"You step out of the house, irrespective of whichever locality you are living in and you are never sure whether you will be able to return home safely," Nadir informs while gnawing on a drumstick.

Burning and destruction of public and private property by angry mobs and strikes soon after any incident have become routine. Crime mafias, collusion between police officers and local mobs, a thriving drug trade and armed militia, illegal immigration and rising poverty, infrastructure and developmental challenges, unemployment and religious fanaticism. Karachi's problems go on and on. But despite all these shortcomings, the city retains its sense of unlimited potential, its aura of being the nation's promised land and for those who love it there will never be an equal.

As Pakistan's largest metropolis and commercial hub, Karachi still has so much good to offer. Though Nadir is looking the other way, at all the negative scenarios that are part and parcel of just about every urban enclave, I'm more inclined to tune into all the trendy restaurants, air conditioned shopping malls and art galleries that we had driven by on our way back from the airport. Stepping outside the airport terminal, I didn't so much as see Karachi as feel it. The sticky sea air was filled with the weight of humidity and it was this feeling more than anything else that took me back to my childhood. Since I left the city relatively young, when I was just eleven and did not return until now, twenty one years later, I didn't get a chance to form a real bond with Karachi. But I still want to claim it and make it mine. If only Nadir would be more reasonable. He has left the dinner table to attend to a phone call, but ten minutes later Nadir returns with a news magazine that he thrusts towards me.

"Well?"

"Well what?"

"Read the article," Nadir commands. "The one about Orangi."

"Now?"

"Now."

"Whatever."

I grudgingly put aside the mangoes I was about to devour. The magazine is crumpled and slightly damp. It's an old issue that came out in 1995 so it's about eight years old and I can't quite understand its significance to my cousin, but I read on.

The article talks about the Orangi Pilot Project, Karachi's most successful example of urban revival and a global model for development. Schools with computer labs and low cost clinics have been set up to provide for the poor. One of the biggest issues that Orangi has dealt with is providing clean water supply to the city's poorer neighborhoods where pipelines were deliberately empty on the behest of Karachi's water mafia. This stirs my interest. I ask Nadir to elaborate.

"Those *gondas* were holding workers at gunpoint if they dared to interfere and restore the water lines," Nadir proclaims. "Of course, our illustrious government has done nothing to maintain law and order and we can't sit around forever waiting for someone to pick up the slack. We have to question the existing situation and make space for our own systems. That's the Karachi way."

Nadir talks about the success of the Citizen-Police Liaison Committee that managed to curb some of the civil violence in the mid 1990's when Karachi was struck with rampant kidnappings and murders on a daily basis. Much of the trouble was stirred by unresolved grievances between the government of then Prime Minister Benazir Bhutto and the Mohajir Qaumi Movement, a political party representing Karachi's immigrants, composing almost 60% of the city's population.

"It was awful," Nadir says. "The whole city was a blood bath. Of course the MQM has always denied it was part of the problem. But if Benazir had really cared about Karachi's slums and rising unemployment, perhaps the MQM wouldn't have found such willing recruits. They exploited the situation to the hilt like all good opportunists."

We argue about who was more responsible for the bloodshed. While I blame the MQM, my cousin finds more fault with Benazir Bhutto's tactics.

"Her way of dealing with the mess was to host *iftar* dinners in Islamabad with journalists and bigwigs in the media. They were all clueless about Karachi's on the ground realities. A *paan* seller in Bori Bazaar would have known more than any of those puffed up intellectuals."

According to Nadir, Benazir had banned six Karachi newspapers for sensationalizing the violence. And yet, she claimed to have a democratic platform.

"What a wasted opportunity," Nadir says and shakes his head. "She was a deeply flawed individual, just like her father. Too much of that feudal Sindhi pride and plain old greed. She simply couldn't get past it."

"What do you think her chances are now?" I ask. "Will she make a comeback?"

"Only with the help of the Americans. And the military of course."

"The military?" I scoff. "I thought she hated those guys."

"She also cannot survive without support from the Generals," Nadir declares. "It has always been this way in our part of the world. The elites like to condemn our top military brass, but they're also profiting by having them in charge. Pakistan's civil-military alliances are bankrolling their villas and their children's fancy schmancy educations."

"So you want Pakistan to continue to be ruled by men in uniform? Isn't that what we need to get away from? How can you seriously support army rule and call yourself progressive?"

"Don't be so silly. Of course I don't support it. I'm just trying to get you to see the big picture. We don't really have too many alternatives. Every civilian leader we've ever had has been as corrupt as the other. Benazir was no exception. She may have a posh accent and be the darling of the West, but as far as I'm concerned, that woman did no good for this country."

I recall Benazir's image on posters and billboards. The fleshy lips stained a rich burgundy, the flawless ivory complexion, the smoldering black eyes and shapely brows, the oversized black framed glasses sliding halfway down that perfectly sloped nose, the transparent white *dupatta* partly covering her ebony tresses. It was all far too glamorous for a Prime Minister. But there was something about Benazir that made me feel proud to be Pakistani.

She had so much poise. And when she spoke, no matter what she said, there was no escaping her presence, her style and sophistication always held me captive and I would stare at her and admire her, not because of her leadership skills, certainly not because of her policies, but because of what she represented. Modernity. Class. Elegance. These are not qualities one associates with Pakistan. But Benazir made me imagine that they were indeed part of the country's mixture as manifested in her persona.

"Well?" says Nadir.

"Well what?"

Our conversation grinds to a halt when we cannot agree on the future of Pakistan's governance. I still want to make a case for Benazir, but Nadir won't listen. He's far too cynical. But not entirely complacent. I detect in him a certain attitude that seems unique to Karachites. It's the mingling of disenchantment with hope. It keeps alive the optimist. It requires a great deal of tolerance. Faith too, but maybe that's just going overboard.

*   *   *

Produce vendors rolling wooden carts the size of pool tables laden with fruit. Custard apples, pomegranates, papayas. *Amroot* for guavas. *Chicoo* ice cream in shades of sand. Buses and minivans honking madly. Plumes of steam rising from hot pavements after a monsoon downpour. Chili peppers wrinkling under the tropical sun. Baby mangoes wrapped in burlap and stowed in tin trunks. Crayola colored laundry flapping in balconies. The sweet smell of *raat ki raani*. Flower sellers hawking garlands of jasmine in the middle of traffic jams. Hot roasted peanuts in newspaper cones.

The images I retain from my childhood in Karachi are bursting with flavor and I long to taste them again. I have brought with me old family photos to spur the wheels of memory. There are camels on the beach and broken sand castles, a *milad* ceremony at home, commemorating the Prophet's birthday. I am sitting next to my mother on a white cotton sheet covered with rose petals. We are surrounded by women with their heads draped in gauzy pastel *dupattas*. I remember these things happening, but my mind draws a blank when I try to focus on the past. The estrangement is both liberating and unsettling.

To ward off the initial jitters of homecoming, I spend most of my time playing tennis with my cousin's eight year old daughter Jaza. When we come home from the Karachi gymkhana, Jaza leads me straight into her bedroom to show me her collection of Barbie dolls. She has named them after the characters in *Friends* and her favorite at the moment is Rachel. One day, Jaza asks me to go swimming with her and I am embarrassed to tell her that I don't know how. She thinks I'm making an excuse.

"But that's so silly! Are you really from America? How can you not know how to swim?"

I explain to Jaza that my parents didn't want me to wear a bathing suit in public, so I had a note from home excusing me from swimming lessons when I was in middle school.

"That's too bad," Jaza says. "Weren't you mad at your parents?"

"Not really," I lie while reliving the agony of sitting alone on the bleachers watching my friends frolic in the pool.

"Well my parents don't care about all those things," she says. "They let me wear anything I like. I am so glad I live in Pakistan!"

As Jaza proceeds to change the outfits of all her Barbies, I think of all the other Jazas I have seen at the gymkhana banging away at the tennis courts in shorts, another item I was strictly forbidden to wear in the States. It didn't mean to suggest that I hadn't assimilated

well after leaving Pakistan for America. In many ways,
upbringing in Karachi, where English was spoken at h
Dancing Queen blared from my stereo, made assimilati   .. less a
moot point. When I came to the United States, no one would have
guessed that I was a foreigner until I opened my mouth and asked
for the *loo* instead of the bathroom or wondered why the lift not the
elevator was taking so long. Once I had asked for directions to the
nearest petrol pump much to the bewilderment of the middle aged
cashier at the grocery store who could scarcely fathom I was only
asking for the gas station.

The peculiar vocabulary as well as my English accent became a
liability especially at school. I was taken for a snob. So I made it my
number one priority in the seventh grade to learn to speak like an
American. Every day after school, I would spend countless hours in
front of the television watching reruns of *Gilligan's Island* and the
Brady Bunch. While I admired Ginger's pretty ball gowns, what I
longed for, more than anything else in the world, was to be able to
mimic Marcia Brady.

By the time I was a high school freshman, I was flouting my
newly acquired American idioms, competing on the tennis team and
also running track. My best friend at the time was an Indian Muslim
nymphet who often questioned my compulsion to wear jeans during
a summer heat wave when everyone else, including herself, was
staying cool in Bermuda shorts and spaghetti strapped sun dresses. I
told my friend that it was a matter of preserving customs from "back
home" which didn't really make a whole lot of sense when the Karachi
girl in me was hardly an example of a uniform cultural identity. If
anything, she was a mishmash of competing cultures, east and west,
Abba, Travolta, and the Quran happily co-existing in the same world.

I never had to make a choice in those days, but having transported
my life halfway across the world, I was expected to retain something
of my roots, and that something would inevitably mutate into a
narrow, stilted version of the original melting pot culture I had grown
up with. Not wearing shorts on hot muggy days made my American
friends think I was a naïve and sheltered Pakistani girl, someone
who had never seen paved roads before and certainly didn't know
the first thing about disco dancing. Or so it was presumed.

* * *

The following day I head to the Sind club for a luncheon with Kamla Aunty. She is an aunt of my mother's, married to Ammi's paternal uncle who had immigrated to Pakistan from India to expand the family's textile business. Ammi had stayed with her aunt when she was visiting Karachi in 1969 after completing her studies in Bombay which was her hometown. In fact, it was at one of Kamla Aunty's Karachi bridge parties where Ammi was noticed and introduced to my future grandmother who was looking for a good match for her one and only son. That, in a nutshell, is how my mother and father met and got married.

Kamla Aunty had held the *nikkah* ceremony in her own house and the old black and white wedding pictures show her standing beside the bride and groom, wearing her trademark sleeveless blouse and crushed silk sari, looking every inch the chic and sophisticated socialite with a fashionable mop of black curls framing her Sophia Loren visage.

In my childhood, I used to spend many happy moments enjoying afternoon tea complete with cucumber sandwiches and rich buttery scones in Kamla Aunty's elegant sitting room and going on shopping excursions with her three daughters. They would spoil me rotten with chili chips and *kulfi* snacks and Kamla Aunty would indulge my love for reading and pile me with books on science and nature while encouraging me to ask her questions about the things I didn't understand or wanted to learn more about. What I liked most about Kamla Aunty was her voice, a soft musical lilt that felt like a soothing balm.

"So good to see you again my dear! What pretty *chappals*. They are absolutely charming."

Ah yes. The same old voice. Unmistakeably Kamla Aunty's. For an instant, I catapult back into time riding in the back seat of her chauffeured Mercedes. I am reading a dog eared copy of Enid Blyton's *Claudine at St. Clare's* and chuckling over the misadventures of the new French girl who gets into all kinds of mischief at an English boarding school. Kamla Aunty's uniformed driver crawls through the busy thoroughfare of Tariq Road where we always went shoe shopping. In those days it was black patent Mary Janes from Bata's that were my staple every school year. Twenty years later, I returned to that very same road only to indulge in hand embroidered sandals from a fancy boutique selling everything from strappy stilettos to knee high boots available in snakeskin or rich creamy leather. I plan to go back to the boutique a dozen more times. A girl could die happy shoe shopping in Karachi.

Kamla Aunty kisses me on both cheeks and flashes a gummy smile. Her maroon stained lips are slightly smeared at the edges, but otherwise she is the picture of style and sophistication in her turquoise chiffon sari and sleeveless blouse. We engage in a light hearted conversation about Pakistani fashions that include slim cut pants paired with above the knee form fitting tunic tops with long side slits. The modern silhouettes make me look like a country bumpkin in my billowing *shalwars* and sack like *kurtas*, about two decades passé. But at least my *chappals* are more fashion forward. Kamla Aunty confers approval, her gaze drifting towards my feet every so often as we talk.

"Of course, the summer outfits are rather frivolous compared to the winter season. There is something so solid about winter clothing. All those rich browns and one can't really go wrong with black or gray. I always told your mother to wear darker colors to complement her fair skin. But she did so love those pastel saris your father would bring back from Hong Kong."

We talk about my parents' stagnating health. I mention they're still working well into their retirement years. Kamla Aunty clucks her tongue with dismay. Something about the look on her face makes me think that life in Pakistan wouldn't have made my parents toil so hard. They would have been able to take it easier, but whether or not they would have been any happier is hard to say.

Kamla Aunty gestures to a white uniformed waiter with a barely noticeable wave. I leave it up to her to order for the two of us and she selects tomato soup and chicken *tikka* with a pitcher of *nimboo pani* or lemonade.

"I'm going to my tailor tomorrow afternoon," says Kamla Aunty. "You are most welcome to come along should you need some new things."

I tell her that I'm saving most of my clothes shopping for Lahore. Kamla Aunty wrinkles her nose and tells me that Karachi styles are by far superior. Her chiffon sari and wedge heeled sandals attest to her sense of style. In fact, she looks even more dignified aging into her seventies and for an instant I recall a crystal clear image of Kamla Aunty's mother whom I had once visited at her Malabar Hill mansion in Bombay. She always had a poodle tucked under one arm and spoke French with her husband. Kamla Aunty has the same high society manners and when our talk veers into more serious matters about Karachi's changing demographics, Kamla Aunty wrinkles her nose and professes disdain for an increasingly regressive, tasteless society.

"What good has come from all those illiterate Pathans migrating into the city," she says rather angrily. "They have brought nothing but trouble with their *charas* and heroin, not to mention their love of guns. The dacoits have free reign and people are beginning to live in ethnic ghettos. It was never this provincial before. Parsis, Christians, Hindus, they all used to get along rather well in Karachi. Even Bombay's not the same anymore. So many of the younger girls have started wearing the *burqa*. Imagine that! The *burqa* of all things. I tell you one thing. We're getting more and more Arabized. We've lost our bearings. But at least we still have this place. It's one of the few sanctuaries in Karachi where one can still relax." Kamla Aunty looks around the ornate surroundings and sighs.

"A bit of an odd place really. So much leftover baggage from the Raj. But you can't really be too hard on the British. Our cultures are deeply intertwined. Just look at Karachi. So much of it was built by the Brits."

I nod and try to recall what my father had said about Karachi. Something along the lines of the wild wild West. A dirty, ramshackle place long past its prime.

The white gloved waiter clears the table and brings desert. I had requested mango ice cream, but he serves us caramel custard with a pot of milky black tea fragrant with cardamom. It's absolutely delicious. Afterwards, Kamla Aunty gives me a brief tour of the club. We walk along the long verandahs wrapped around the building and pass elegant gardens with enormous hibiscus blooms, tennis and squash courts, the main dining hall, a formal living room, a card room in which to play bridge, a reading room and a cocktail bar. The furnishings are old world colonial style with fabrics and carpets in muted earth tones, black and white village prints, and polished silver cups and trophies.

It's all very civilized and genteel and utterly strange. I can't get too comfortable here. I keep thinking about what lies beyond the club's high walls and black wrought iron gate, the sheer turmoil and chaos of Karachi's streets, the city's throbbing pulse, all its squalor and grit and vivaciousness that I have to come to rely upon as a daily tonic.

Kamla Aunty points out the Sind spelling, the old British version, even though everywhere else in the country the province is known as Sindh. She tells me that when the club was founded in 1871, there were about seventy five members, all British civil servants. Indian and Pakistani members were not accepted until the early to mid 1950's.

"Why don't you stay here for a few days while you're in Karachi?" Kamla Aunty inquires. "They have residential quarters on the first floor. It can easily be arranged."

"I'm not sure how much longer I will be here," I reply. "But thank you so much for lunch. It's been wonderful to see you again after all these years."

"You're most welcome my dear. Do drop by the flat anytime you wish."

Kamla Aunty calls for her chauffeur and offers to drop me back at Nadir's house, but I tell her to go on without me as I want to take my time getting back.

"As you wish dear," Kamla Aunty responds.

I watch her hike up the ends of her sari to climb inside an aging but well preserved Mercedes. And then, just when I thought I wouldn't see it again, Kamla Aunty flashes that trademark smile, so similar to Sophia Loren's.

*   *   *

Like other big cities in the world, Karachi is a composite of many different layers. The average first time visitor sees only its top most surface, the city's most unsavory and off putting elements. Getting used to all the noise and crowds is another matter, something you either crave or detest. Then you have to figure out how to get around town. Walking is not practical. You're likely to get killed, either by a person, moving vehicle or the wrath of a sun that knows no mercy. Subways are unheard of. Public buses are not recommended unless you don't particularly mind losing your flip flops in the mad scramble to climb on board or stapling yourself to the person next to you for a good half hour or so. Driving in Karachi could be lethal or a pure joy ride depending on your skill. I did not have the guts to try any of the above.

Leaving the Sind club, I hail a taxi and tell the driver to head towards Karachi Development Authority, better known as KDA, via a long and circuitous route. I'm in the mood to take some pictures and just feast on the visual banquet of Karachi's streets that are as vibrant as ever, befuddling the newcomer with stark dualities, glitzy versus primitive, modern versus medieval, opulence versus poverty. In some ways, Karachi reminds me so much of New York City where I've always felt at home.

Perhaps it's because of that familiar electrifying buzz in the air or the smorgasbord of ethnicities representing the city's myriad faces. Karachi's multicultural population includes Sindhi, Makrani, Kashmiri, Punjabi, Parsi, Baloch, Pashtun. Among Muslims there are not just Sunnis and Shias, but further sub sects such as Boris, Memons, Khojas, Ismailis, Ahmadis. Though the Hindu and Christian populations are nowhere near what they were pre-partition, every once in a while I will glimpse some vestiges of the past like an old Anglican church or the Gandhi Gardens Zoo where I used to play hide and seek as a child and where Jackie Kennedy had visited when she was touring Karachi in 1962 as First Lady.

It was hardly the first time that Karachi had hosted an American celebrity. Back in the 1950's, Karachi was strongly influenced by Western pop culture. It was the height of the cold war and the United States and the Soviet Union were engaged in a fierce turf battle to see who could put on the best shows and draw the biggest crowds.

One of the most celebrated performances was Dizzy Gillespie's concert at Karachi's Palace Cinema in 1956. The eighteen-piece American jazz band was on its first leg of a ten week Asian tour and played for three consecutive nights in Karachi. My father had attended the concert and he still talks about it as though it had happened yesterday. He talks about the mad rush to buy tickets, about Dizzy's signature trumpet with its bent bell, about the impromptu jam session when one of the audience members hopped on stage to play with the band. There had also been a live broadcast over Pakistani radio. Tickets for the half-hour radio show were sold out within fifteen minutes. Dizzy and his crew were special guests at Karachi's International Women's Club where they had been invited for tea.

"I'm nervous as a hep cat," one of the band members reportedly said.

Overseen by the State Department during the Eisenhower administration, the Musical Ambassadors project aimed to broaden America's prestige and influence abroad, particularly in the Near and Middle East. American government officials embraced these public diplomacy tours in places like Karachi and Kabul, to promote good will and better understanding of the United States. Dizzy's sellout performance in Karachi was clearly the winner compared to the Soviet-sponsored troupe of singers, dancers and acrobats that passed through town the year before attracting just a handful of guests to the Embassy, whereas the American jazz crew had taken over one of Karachi's largest movie theaters with standing room only capacity.

It was a gentler, subtler form of US foreign policy in action, operationally significant in relying on non-state actors to further geo-political aims. The choice of artists invited to tour overseas scored high on personality factors. Despite having dodged the draft in World War II, Dizzy Gillespie had the honor of being one of the first jazz musicians to represent the United States on a cultural mission. He ended up collaborating with local artists in Karachi and creating his own lick on their scale. A raga entitled Rio Pakistan.

Dave Brubeck followed suit when he came to Karachi two years after Dizzy making an album in 1958 called *Jazz Impressions of Eurasia.*

In his New York Times article *The Beat Heard Around the World,* Brubeck made the case for the social impact of music and its power to transcend language, culture and race.

"Jazz," he wrote "arouses a kinship among peoples; it affords them flashes of recognition of common origins."

In addition to Dizzy Gillespie, Karachi also hosted The Duke Ellington Band fresh from the success of performances in Beirut,

Baghdad and Tehran. Jack Teagarden had played the trombone at the Rex Cinema Hall. Shortly after that, it was Artie Shaw on his clarinet. This intersection of art with foreign affairs exposed Pakistan to a greater influx of US culture that shaped a whole generation of Karachites growing up during the 1950's.

In addition to jazz, Hollywood movies were also big at that time. Karachi was a cinephile's Mecca where the ardent Pakistani picture goer could spend days ensnared in the city's darkened movie theaters watching everything from Fred Astaire musicals to Spaghetti Westerns and Hitchcock thrillers.

A French Riviera by the Arabian Sea, a carefree, happening town exuding cosmopolitan cool. This was once the face of Karachi, a face that will never come back, no matter how much you long for it.

The cabbie is now winding around the narrow alleys just off of McLeod Road. We pass camels and donkey carts and the streets get narrower and are lined with market stalls where almost anything might be available. As in the Middle Eastern *souq*, products are categorized into specific bazaars. The Sarafa Bazaar is known for silver. Khajoor Bazaar for dates. Bori Bazaar is where my grandmother used to buy fabrics for her caftans. And then there is Saddar Bazaar, a rambunctious rabbit's warren offering everything from copper, brass, cloth, jewelry, and food.

I don't want to go to Saddar just yet. I'm saving it for another day, hoping to be able to visit the Saddar house I grew up in as a child, but I have no idea who lives there now and how my presence there will be received.

We're approaching Zainab Market which remains just the same as I remember it. There is that unmistakable electricity in the air, the hustle and bustle of commerce, narrow alleyways packed with shoppers and busy vendors selling textiles, carpets and rugs. This is the place for handicrafts. The taxi pulls to a stop and I zip inside the market and prowl through the stalls searching for old Sindhi fabrics and maybe a hand dyed block printed chador.

I am in luck for I come to a shop that has all these and much much more. I set aside some embroidered cushion covers embellished with dime sized mirrors and eye a stack of rainbow hued Pashmina scarves. They'll do nicely as gifts. The vendor entices me with some lapis lazuli jewelry and I fall in love with a tribal necklace with a large square shaped pendant set around smaller blue stones and some silver. I buy it as an early birthday gift for myself.

"*Shukria.*"

The shopkeeper thanks me for the purchases and gives me his card. Then he calls for his assistant, a small boned boy no more than ten, to carry my packages to the waiting taxi. I make a mental note of returning to Sindhi Crafts Emporium to stock up on more treasures. Shopping is turning out to be one of my biggest pleasures in Pakistan. The variety of merchandise, their quality and prices are among the best I have seen anywhere in the world.

"*Aur agay chalo,*" I tell my driver. "*Amreekan markaz kay taraf.*"

He speeds up along Abdullah Haroon Road, passing by a row of palm trees and stops by the American Consulate. I knew the place as an urban oasis that had an excellent library and cafeteria open to the public. But the building looks so different now surrounded with razor wire and pocked with shrapnel from frequent attacks. Nonetheless, this is where it all started, my *hijrah* from Pakistan to America, that flight of migration from the known world to the unknown. My grandmother was the first to leave since her visa paperwork was completed one year ahead in 1981.

It was a dark time for Pakistan. The country was under martial law instigated by President/General Zia ul Haq. To further legitimize his authority, Zia took on the mantle of religion hammering out zealous policies that were supposedly Islamic in order to bolster unilateral support for an unelected military regime.

We never really felt the brunt of these policies on a personal day to day level. Our family life in Pakistan just hummed along on its own course while the political dramas played out their shenanigans. But we knew that the country was changing and not all the changes were positive.

There was concern that I may not to be able to learn English at school if all the subjects were taught in Urdu. Change was imminent when my school added a new unit in religion known as Islamiat. It also became compulsory to learn Sindhi, the provincial language of Karachi's Sindh province. There was no practical reason for this. It was just about as pointless as fifth graders in Harlem being forced to take Latin. The revised school curriculum weakened my thirst for learning. I wanted to skip classes and spend more time reading my own books. I was captivated with stories and folklore about Native Americans and the Indian princess Sacajawea. It was through these stories that I began to feel a yearning for America. I imagined it as a place of thick green forests with mountains and streams and wide open spaces. I dreamed of wearing moccasins and playing inside a teepee. It was a child's fantasy, my escape from a Pakistan that was no longer desirable.

There was always some nuisance to put up with like the numerous power cuts that would last for days and nothing could be done other than waiting and making do with candlelight and paper fans in the stifling heat. Some days, entire sections of Karachi would shut down because of a *hartal*, when people protested against the government by strikes creating all sorts of inconveniences. You couldn't just step out for some shopping or hail a taxi or have dinner at your favorite restaurant or even find a doctor's office that was open for business.

We're approaching the east end of M.A. Jinnah Road, a busy thoroughfare of taxis, rickshaws, buses, motorcycles, cars, pedestrians and rickety wooden carts pulled by donkeys or camels. The driver passes by the white marbled mausoleum of Pakistan's founding father, Muhammad Ali Jinnah. As though by instinct, he knows this is a stopping point and finds a shady spot near a makeshift sidewalk shop where a teenage girl is selling towels and hair combs and bottles of Suave shampoo spread out on a blanket. I make my way towards the spacious gardens encircling Jinnah's *mazar*. It is a lively place filled with boys playing cricket, families picnicking, friends gossiping, couples stealing precious minutes.

My thoughts drift towards Jinnah. Despite championing the making of Pakistan, he never really wanted the "moth ridden" country that was carved out of India on the eve of British departure, but saw it as the only solution to safeguard the minority rights of Indian Muslims clamoring for a separate homeland. Jinnah's vision for Pakistan spoke of an inclusive and pluralist democracy promising equal rights for all citizens regardless of religion, caste or creed. The country's creation was his dying political achievement for he passed away a year later in 1948, leaving behind a utopian vision that was never fully implemented.

Had Jinnah lived longer, Pakistan may at least have had the chance to sustain astute statesmanship and develop stronger political institutions, the lack of which has handicapped the country throughout its chequered history. Apart from its bad luck with leaders, Pakistan has also had the misfortune of geography being situated in the middle of the world's biggest uncertainties where it is both a player and a victim. Unlike India, which is rooted in its soil, Pakistan is an experimental country, born out of ideals. It was a tall order for any nation state to be a beacon of social justice, happy and prosperous with its diverse band of citizens free to live and work as they pleased. The experiment went horribly awry. Jinnah should have lowered his sights.

As I leave the mausoleum and climb back into my taxi, it occurs to me that Pakistan was never meant to be a country at all. It should never have happened. It was a colossal blunder. The gap between the ideal and the real is just so wide and impossible to bridge. But it's far too late now.

* * *

Though Karachi's doomsday image is well entrenched in the limelight of international politics, the city's history is anything but one dimensional. Legend has it that Karack Bunder was an important trading harbor on the Arabian Sea in the late seventeenth and early eighteenth centuries. When the estuary silted up due to heavy rains, the merchants of Karack Bunder, many of whom were Hindus, decided to relocate their activities to what is modern day Karachi. In 1729, they built a fortified settlement on high ground and surrounded it with a mud and timber-reinforced wall over sixteen feet high which had gun-mounted turrets and a gate facing the sea known as Kharadar, or salt gate.

The settlement was strategically located and well protected. There were mangrove marches to the east, the sea to the west and southwest, and the Lyari River to the north. Karachi, then known as Kolachi for a fisherman's wife who had set out on her own to retrieve her husband at sea when all the villagers refused to cooperate, housed monuments of both Hindu and Muslim significance. Among them was the temple of Mahadev, mentioned in the epic Ramayana, where Ram and Sita are supposed to have spent a night on the way to Baluchistan, the tombs of Abdullah Shah and his brother Yousef Shah, both tenth century Sufi saints, and the twelfth century tomb and monastery of Manghopir. Now absorbed and forgotten among the hubbub of metropolitan Karachi, these ancient sites had attracted large numbers of pilgrims from the interior of Sindh, Kutch, Rajasthan and the western coast of India, long before the formation of Pakistan.

In the mid eighteen hundreds, the Great Game rivalry between Britain and Czarist Russia led to the occupation of Karachi by British troops as a landing port during the first Anglo-Afghan war. The so called Army of the Indus ventured into Afghanistan with a total of 16,500 men, including cooks, blacksmiths, water carriers, as well as servants to polish brass and wash clothes. Each regiment used two camels just to carry their cigars and a Brigadier had sixty camels for his own personal luggage. The expedition resulted in a humiliating defeat for the British. One lone survivor returned with his body slumped over his horse, a fitting reminder of the quatrain by Rudyard Kipling:

> "....when you're wounded and left on Afghanistan's plains,
> and the women come out to cut up what remains,
> jest roll to your rifle and blow out your brains,
> and go to your Gawd like a soldier..."

To reclaim the empire's standing after the Afghan defeat, the British annexed the province of Sindh in 1843 under the command of General Charles Napier. He considered it "an advantageous, useful, humane piece of rascality" and upon dismantling the local ruler, the province of Sindh became part of the British India's Bombay Presidency and Karachi was made into district headquarters. Napier eventually made Karachi the capital of Sindh and declared, "You will yet be the glory of the East; would that I could come again, Karachi to see you in your grandeur."

From a garrison town for the English, Karachi went on to become one of the centers of global commerce under the British East India

Trading Company aided by the completion of the Sindh Railway in 1861, which linked Karachi to the agricultural heartland of the Punjab and northern India. At the same time the British began the development of irrigation schemes that brought large desert areas under cultivation and increased activity at Karachi's port. By 1868, Karachi became the largest exporter of wheat and cotton in British India. It was during this period that the British constructed important civic buildings and churches all over Karachi.

The first church was built in 1843 and is still in use today as the assembly hall of St. Joseph's Convent School. In 1885, a public tramway was introduced in Karachi. It was owned by the East India Tramway Company and functioned on steam power that was replaced by horse-drawn carriages in 1892 when Karachiites objected to the noise made by the steam locomotives that were apparently scaring the animals which were then used for transport purposes.

During the First World War, Karachi became a military base as it was the first port of call for ships coming through the Suez and the gateway to the Russian Empire north of Afghanistan. In 1924, one of the first airports in British India was constructed in Karachi and a nascent tourist industry developed around the city's healthy seaside climate that was considered most suitable for patients of asthma and TB.

To this day, Karachi's colonial architecture remains a glorious testament to its commercialism and importance under the Raj. My favorite of these is the lushly ornate Frere Hall named for Sir Bartle Frere, who was governor of the Bombay Presidency in the late 1800's. Made with buff, grey and red limestone, the hall's octagonal tower, columned arches and sloping roof give it a distinct Venetian look, artsy and elegant. During British rule, it was used for civic purposes such as lectures, concerts, stage productions and town hall meetings.

These days, Frere Hall's most conspicuous visitors are a flock of pigeons roaming through the grassy lawns and though the building now houses a library with countless rare books, I am astonished to discover less than ten people there, which makes Frere Hall far more popular with the birds. Nonetheless, it remains an imposing structure and impossible to miss, the European look seamlessly blending in with Karachi's eclectic skyline of east meets west.

The site that intrigues me the most is the Ratneshwar Mahadev Hindu temple at Clifton. It was originally a cave some thirty to forty feet in the sea. When it was constructed as a temple, about two hundred year ago, it contained no idols, only an oil lamp. You could meditate there and I rather like this idea of sitting calmly in a sea cave temple listening to the waves and trying to find your center.

Interestingly, there were more Hindus living in Karachi than Muslims before the 1947 partition of British India that resulted in the creation of Pakistan. By the mid 1950's, millions of Indian Muslim migrants known as *mohajirs* poured into Karachi either overland from the Sindh-Rajasthan border or by sea which is how my father arrived as a fifteen year old boy from Bangalore on board the passenger ship, the *SS Damra*.

There was a huge shortage of housing for these new immigrants. Large communities of make shift huts sprang up in a matter of months for the poorer refugees amidst a construction boom from low interest housing loans. Some of Karachi's oldest neighborhoods were developed by the government such as Nazimabad where the bulk of residents originated from Delhi from the state of Uttar Pradesh in Northern India. Language was their key contribution, a chaste almost courtly form of Urdu that eventually became the lingua franca of Karachi.

Along with language, food was also a major component of this Indo-Pakistani cultural fusion. Karachiites could now find delicacies native to each migrant community like *bagharey baingan*, a piquant eggplant dish cooked in the Hyderabadi style, they could buy pastries from Ambala Sweets, bread from Aligarh Bakery, snacks and savories from Lucknow Chat House, kebabs from Meerut Kabab House. None of these places exist now, but in the early days of Karachi's formation, the connection with India was quite strong.

If partition was the first layer that revamped the look and feel of Karachi, changing the city's demographics with a majority of Indian Muslim migrants, then the war in Afghanistan during the Soviet occupation from 1979-88 was another dramatic facelift. The aftermath brought the largest number of Afghan refugees anywhere in the world into Pakistan, estimated over three million, many of whom settled in Karachi to find jobs and housing which were already in short supply. The Afghans built communities like Sohrab Goth, where everyone speaks Pashto and Kabul is not just on the other side of the mountains, but alive and well in the heart of Karachi. According to a UN report, there will be more than twenty million people living in Karachi by the year 2015 making it one of the world's mega cities, a very different outcome from the muddy fishing village it once inhabited over three hundred years ago.

*   *   *

"The KSE broke another record today," Nadir announces when he picks me up from the Gulf Shopping Center in Clifton. He throws an amused glance at the pile of shopping bags I shove into the back seat of the car. "Cleaned out the mall, eh?"

Nadir winks and thrusts a newspaper in my hand to distract me from Karachi's rush hour traffic, a road circus that has often reminded me of the modern day version of Ben Hur, with Toyotas, Mazdas, Hondas, Kawasakis and Yamahas substituting for chariots. We circle past the *teen talwar* monument at a busy traffic island in Clifton. It's a striking piece of architecture, its name indicating three marble swords jutting heavenwards, their pristine whiteness contrasting against the chambray blue sky. Nadir tells me that each sword is inscribed with the words Unity, Faith and Discipline, the nation's founding creed. He says this with so much fervor and earnestness that for a minute I am fully convinced that Nadir still believes these lofty words apply to a country that couldn't be further removed from its ideals. It turns out that he does.

"What do you think of the article?" Nadir asks.

"What article?"

"The one about the KSE index. I thought it was right up your alley."

I scan the newspaper in my lap and come across a headline that reads *Karachi Soars*. According to the article, the Karachi Stock Exchange reached a new high on the KSE-100 Index with a record turnover of over nine hundred million shares on August 7, 2003, accumulating a market capitalization of a staggering $17 billion. The article mentions that the KSE has been rated one of the world's best performing emerging markets, comprising more than seven hundred companies listed on the exchange. Analysts predict a healthy market forecast.

"You ought to write a story about that," Nadir chimes in. "I can hook you up with my friend Saqib. He'll give you more stats on the economy. He's a whiz at numbers. Last I heard, he was going to accept an offer from Goldman Sach's in Manhattan, but he's decided to stay put in Karachi for a while. You'll enjoy meeting him. He went to Wharton for his MBA."

While we've come to a miraculous stop at a red light, my cousin unearths a gadget from the front pocket of his jeans and proceeds to browse thru his contact list as he steers with one hand, his attention span flip flopping from the road to the small LCD display of his organizer.

"Here, take this down."

I scribble a mobile phone number on the edge of the newspaper and a hotmail address.

"He's a good guy," Nadir continues. "Doesn't mess around with any BS. But do us both a favor and stay away from politics. Saqib is a finance man. He won't want to get bogged down with all your talk about Zia and Bhutto and all the other ghosts from the past."

I look out the window pretending to be deaf.

"Look, I'm sorry," Nadir says. "All I'm saying is that there is no room for hashing out politics when you're discussing the economy."

"Is that so?" I reply somewhat tersely. "Try telling that to all those foreign investors afraid to step foot into Pakistan because of what they see on the nightly news. You may want to talk stock quotes, but all they're thinking are bomb blasts."

As we crawl thru traffic, Nadir goes on and on about the rising stock market, GDP growth, lower interest rates, rising exports and a steady influx of foreign remittances from Pakistani workers abroad that have contributed to a robust economy fueled by President Musharraf's aggressive privatization program. What is not so clear is whether the self appointed leader of Pakistan will be as successful on the political front in curbing the domestic terrorism jeopardizing the nation's economic prowess. Nadir dismisses my idea that Karachi has a split personality, a microcosm of a country vacillating between extremes, modernity and fanaticism, showcasing two entirely different Pakistans. Both versions have validity.

Nonetheless, Pakistan's economic growth story has been largely muffled out by global security concerns and perceptions of wide spread instability. Positive factors undermined by negatives. It's totally understandable. And yet, and yet, there are so many things here that throw you off guard. Like that billboard we just passed with a Pakistani Catherine Zeta Jones lookalike gushing over a cell phone. Or the Vespas that overtake us with an entire family on two wheels. A toddler stands up front holding onto the handlebars. Behind the husband/driver is his wife side saddled with one or more babies bouncing on her lap. How the whole lot manages to hang onto their dear lives and survive the anarchy that is Karachi traffic with no seatbelts and infant car seats is utterly beyond me.

When we arrive back at the house, Nadir's mother is lounging on the sofa reading fashion magazines. I immediately make a beeline and we divvy up a stash of thick glossy volumes and ooh and ah over the ankle length skirts known as *lenghas* in silk and chiffon with sequined tunics and lacy *dupattas*. Jewelry ads feature earrings and chokers in intricate cuts of diamonds, sapphires, rubies and emeralds. Beaded purses, stiletto heels and evening wraps add a dash of pizzazz. The Pakistani models displaying the elegant wedding attire are downright stunning and sexy. For the next few days, I become addicted to the contents of *Libaas* magazine and the fall designer collections aired on GEO TV.

One by one, a slew of gaunt faced fashionistas sashay down the runway. They have Muslim names like Amina, Nabila, Iraj and Iman. And they are some of the most beautiful faces I have ever seen. It gets all the more alluring with bare backs and midriffs and sumptuous fabrics choreographed to techno beats and the strains of Sting's *Desert Rose*. Suraya Aunty can't understand my sudden fascination with Karachi's catwalk scene.

"It is nothing new," she says. "Surely you have heard of Freiha Altaf?"

I shake my head as though mute, unable to take my eyes off the gorgeous models on television.

Suraya Aunty turns down the volume and tells me about a Pakistani supermodel who rose to worldwide fame in the 1980's, ironically at a time when women's dress and appearance was under more scrutiny in Pakistan given the stringent Islamization campaign waged by General Zia. Defying the stereotyped image of veiled submission, Frieha Altaf also managed to become a successful business woman who formed her own company known as Catwalk. The first of its kind, Catwalk choreographed and produced fashion shows, music concerts and events. Clients included not just major fashion designers, but global corporate clients such as Motorola, Coca Cola, Kodak and Revlon.

I am beginning to have high hopes for the modeling careers of Vaneeza and company. But then an inadvertent change of channels submerges me in a whole other world, where the only thing visible is a sea of veils. A tall and stately woman in full *niqab* stands behind a lectern. Pale blue eyes shimmer above the black patch of cloth shielding her face. She speaks in a smoothly modulated British accent while delivering a Power Point presentation extolling the virtues of Islam. The camera pans over the audience. Women both young and old are hanging on to her every word like stage struck groupies.

"Who is she?" I ask.

"That," says Suraya Aunty with a hardened smile "is none other than Doctor Farhat Hashmi."

A few days later, I attend one of Dr. Hashmi's lectures at a five star hotel. There is an eerie silence as she takes to the podium and begins to recite a verse from the Quran in a mellow yet powerful voice. The majority of her audience are society ladies, accustomed to marathon shopping sprees in air conditioned malls and lazy poolside lunches. They are wearing expensive makeup and designer headscarves.

Dr. Hashmi lectures about the importance of returning to Islamic values.

"The expectations of Pakistanis have not been fulfilled in our fifty-odd years of independence. There is a feeling of betrayal and despair. The transformation begins with ourselves."

Heads are nodding in euphoric single minded approval. I look at the women around me. They seem to be mesmerized by the speaker at the podium whose black veiled face reminds me of masked dancers at a Masquerade ball. Only I can't figure out to what tune this mask is dancing to and why.

"When people benefit from something, they will be drawn to it," Dr. Hashmi says ever so softly in her posh English accent.

And then it dawns on me. Fundo Chic. Consider it the newest trend among Pakistan's urban bourgeoisie. A dose of excitement. Religious enlightenment. A search for direction and newfound guidance. Farhat Hashmi comprises all these elements to her fan club. I find her teachings too narrow, endorsing a conservative brand of Islam, simply cloistering women behind a veil as a badge of piety for public display and topping it off by doing all the interpretation and thinking for her devotees rather than letting them use their own intellect and reason as stipulated in the Quran.

There are soft murmurs and bustling and moving as the women rise from their chairs and circulate around the room. Farhat Hashmi has concluded her lecture. She's still at the podium surrounded by a small platoon of her admirers of Born Again Muslims.

I have trouble sleeping that night. There's a meteor shower in my head. All the disparate elements of Karachi are breaking into small pieces and colliding with each other. Schizophrenia. That's what Karachi has revealed. So many mixed signals and extreme situations. Stock quotes and bomb blasts. Burqas to catwalks. Why is it so hard to find a middle ground in this place?

*   *   *

"COME ON!" Nadir shouts. "Let's go before this miserable heat zaps all our energy."

"Coming coming!"

I emerge from the kitchen having filled up my water bottle. I've been drinking gallons in this summer time blaze, which in Karachi is made worse by the humidity and prickliness that seeps into your pores, making your skin so clammy that you feel like a limp piece of seaweed for the better part of the day and there's nothing you can do except to put up with it. My time in Karachi has more than adequately proven that the American in me is no longer built for this place. The rivers of sweat on my body are a daily reminder.

At least the air conditioner in Nadir's Honda Civic is working again. I won't have to visit our former home in Saddar looking like a half drowned rat. Home. Home! I'm almost there. *Jaldi, jaldi.* Faster, faster. No wait. Slow down. Sloow. Slooooow.

It's ten in the morning and Nadir is moving at a pace much too fast for my memory lane flashbacks. He whizzes by Mama Parsi, my childhood alma mater that still looks like a serene fortress amid the manic traffic on Bunder Road. St. Patrick's where my Dad went to high school is just a red bricked blur and soon we are passing by a row of shoe stores on Tariq Road, the famous English Boot House and my beloved Bata's.

"What's that?"

Nadir glances at my lap where I'm cradling the latest Time magazine with Karachi on the cover, ceremoniously dubbed as a dangerous mess. The article goes on to describe the city's "stable of killers" and how they move up the ladder of "Murder, Inc." From hired assassins to ethnic feuds to systemic corruption among bureaucrats, police and gang members, Karachi's portrayal is dark and dismal. Nadir has read the article which he dismisses as rubbish.

"There you have it," my cousin says. "The Western media wants the world to know that all Karachiites are terrorists and this is a land of outlaws."

My mind flashes back to those uber cool hipsters at the rave. Terrorists indeed. Very dangerous outlaws. At least there had been a mention in the article of Karachi's pampered elite, right down to the tight jeaned girls in Channel sunglasses and the private bashes in high walled mansions. But the bulk of the article was about the city's mean streets. It would be hard to believe that in this "sea of anarchy" there was once any semblance of order and civility.

During colonial times, Karachi's Saddar district was a booming commercial area catering to the needs of the British army who had troops stationed in the Saddar Cantonment. Saddar Bazaar, an exclusive shopping area, consisted of wide roads on a grid plan with residential neighborhoods dominated by Goans, Parsis and Europeans, who owned many of the local businesses. The area surrounding the bazaar was dominated by churches, missionary schools, community halls and civic buildings owned and operated by trusts belonging to Christians (local and Europeans) and Parsi merchants. To the southeast of Saddar Bazaar were the spruced up Civil Lines where the British officers lived and worked and had their clubs. There were celebrations for Christmas, New Year and Easter as well as fancy dress up balls complete with a live band and white gloved waiters serving appetizers and cocktails on polished silver platters.

It was likely that our house on 99/B Depot Lines would have been used for one of those balls. The living room or sitting room as we used to call it had high ceilings and double hinged doors on both sides of the room, leading into the front garden and a large adjoining room that looked like a formal dining hall with a built in sideboard, but was used as my parents' bedroom.

It is almost dark by the time we make it out to Saddar. Then I see the familiar 99/B chiseled into the wall and have my bearings at last. This is it. I have come home. The iron gate by the entrance has rusted with age. But wait. There is a man at the gate shouting for us to leave. Nadir gets out of the car trying to look authoritative. He makes the mistake of telling the man that I have come all the way from America to see the house where I used to live. This only makes the man more defensive and he gets more and more furious, yelling at the top of his lungs.

"*Kya manghte ho? Yahan kuch naheen hay. Chale jao! Jao! Jao!*"

What do you want? There is nothing here. Go away! Scram! Get lost!

He is clearly afraid of us. Maybe he thinks we will report him to the police. I wonder what he's hiding. Nadir makes a few half hearted threats and then backs down when the man's anger shows no signs of abating. When Nadir resorts to a bribe, the man gets more enflamed, sputtering more accusations. We are getting nowhere.

I stretch tall and stand on my tippy toes to glimpse something of the house, but there's not much that's visible outside the gate. All I can make out are some red terra cotta tiles on the rooftop. I am longing to see the latticed verandah with the bamboo shades where I once sat in a wicker rocking chair holding my baby brother. I want to walk across the garden where my grandmother and I laid out our prayer rugs side by side and she taught me how to say *namaz*. I recall the enormous dirt compound where I learned to ride my first bicycle before ramming it into the pointy back fenders of my father's steel gray Fiat. It had round headlights the size of flying saucers and stood in a makeshift garage with four wooden posts and a corrugated tin roof. I picture my pet goat tied up to a *neem* tree and how heartbroken I was when they took her away to be slaughtered for the *Eid* festivities.

If only this obstinate man will let me through. He has disappeared now and I'm facing a brick wall with no one in sight. But someone is there, someone I haven't seen until now, a small beggar boy with a torn shirt and stumps at his elbows. He has witnessed the whole shouting match and now he tells me why I am not allowed inside. It's a squatter's community. Apparently, they are quite enterprising. One fellow has set up a barber shop in what used to be my bedroom. There is another guy who fries *pakoras*, chickpea dumplings in the verandah and bakes fresh bread in a *tandoor* clay oven installed in the old garden.

"*Such hai, yay such hai!*"

The little beggar boy insists he is telling the truth. I can't bear to look him in the eyes, but I know he's not fibbing. A chickpea vendor. A barber. Quite an ambitious lot as far as squatters go. It's a shame I don't get to take any pictures.

*   *   *

In his book, *Travels with Herodotus*, the late Polish writer and journalist, Rycard Kapucinski, weaves epic voyages going back over a thousand years with his own dispatches from around the globe. The result is a fascinating collage of travel and memory, offering a nuanced world view that informs as well as entertains. In one of his passages, Kapucinski writes:

> *The Greek historian and voyager Herodotus was obsessed with memory, fearful on its behalf. He felt that memory is something defective, fragile, impermanent, illusory. That*

whatever it contains, whatever it is storing, can evaporate, simply vanish without a trace. His whole generation, everyone living on earth at that time, was possessed by that same fear. Without memory one cannot live, for it is what elevates man above beasts, determines the contours of the human soul: and yet it is at the same time so unreliable, elusive, treacherous.

I am beginning to concur with these sentiments as I linger in Karachi, my memories becoming an invisible travel companion requiring constant attention, if only to be coddled into believing that their existence still matters. It has been a new experience to be traveling with memories. They make me wrestle with conflicting emotions, to reconcile what I am seeing with what I had experienced long ago. The Pakistan of my childhood is no longer visible. So what does one do when memories clash with reality? And how do you go about validating a past that contradicts all that we know of the present?

I am desperate to believe that there is a Pakistan beyond danger and violence, the country that I am exploring in all its numerous shades and flavors is so much richer than the one depicted on news reports. There is so much to absorb, explain, research, debate and yet, I recoil against analysis. That is not why I have returned after twenty one years. I am here because like Herodotus, I too have an obsession with memory, and if I cannot confirm the old version, then I will need to make a newer one.

6

A ROYAL CARAVAN

Karakoram Highway, July 2003

TWO YOUNG BOYS ARE STANDING by the roadside laughing and waving in our direction. The vehicle I am riding in hugs the edge of a highway that drops a thousand feet below into a deep river gorge. As I look outside my window, I can see the front wheel tracing the rim of the road with centimeters to spare. One of the lads is shouting something and then he cups his hand and flips it toward the ground while laughing uproariously. It is his way of wishing us well, the gestures daring our Winnebago to turn over and fall into the abyss.

I uncross my legs and lean across the aisle to take the triangle shaped chicken *tikka* sandwich from the prince's mother and widow of the late Mir. Her gnarled old face has the texture of distressed leather hide. I'm guessing her age somewhere in the mid eighties. When she smiles at me, her eyes sparkle and shine as though they are attached to a thousand light bulbs. There is no doubting her youthful vitality, her zest for living. She looks at me with curiosity but without judgment. The precise mechanics of why I am here and who I am do not seem to matter to her. And now she is smiling again and offering me another sandwich. Eat, eat, her eyes are saying. You need nourishment. It's going to be a long journey.

There is so much I could ask her, but I don't know where to start, so I end up saying nothing and just keep staring out the window at all this stupendous mind numbing scenery. I have never seen mountains like these. Grey slag heaps of the earth's protruding gut, monuments of stone, wrinkle-skinned like rhinos and elephants, primeval and scabby, capped with icy crags.

I had more or less given up on this excursion. Guided tours were out of the question because of my meager budget and also because they would take away the spirit and excitement of traveling on my own wits. Then I received an email that blew me away.

> *Please proceed to Islamabad ASAP. Mir Saab has expired.*
> *Family will be heading to the palace in Nagar. You may*
> *accompany them as far as Gilgit and make your way from*
> *there into the NA. Adam Khan will be your guide. He's*
> *the Mir's grand nephew. A very nice young man. You*
> *will be in good hands. See you soon. Regards, S.M.*

Major Salim Malik. It was a name scribbled on a grubby paper napkin along with a hotmail address and phone number. I hadn't thought much of that napkin when it was handed to me three months ago in a Boston pub by a colleague from school. But soon after arriving in Pakistan, I had written to the Major, hoping against all hope that he would turn out to be real.

The Major was real alright. And if the contents of his cryptic message were believable, he was making a most tantalizing offer to visit the Northern Areas of Pakistan, a truly lackluster name for a region that can only be described in superlatives.

They call it the rooftop of the world. A meeting point of the Himalayas, Pamirs, Karakoram and Hindu Kush mountain ranges, congregating as hulking giants of jagged saw toothed ridges, towering over twenty thousand feet, the result of a tectonic collision millions of years ago. Now that the Major had come through for me, I had no choice but to follow course. I was absolutely convinced that I had to do this. To travel in the company of absolute strangers to a place right out of a fairy tale. So that was my exit plan from Karachi. I didn't have much to go on. The death of a Mir. A palace. And a boy named Adam Khan.

One of the princes looks out of his binoculars and unleashes a low wolf whistle. I feel like I need to follow up with something equally enthusiastic, but I don't want to come across as too eager less they take me for a common tourist, so I play it cool as if I'm used to stupendous mind numbing scenery in my everyday surroundings. In addition to what's outside the bus, the contents inside are just as intriguing.

I scarcely know anything about the family members of our traveling party on board, a close knit clan of royal sons, daughters, in-laws, and grandchildren. From what I've read in local guide books, they are the torch bearers of an ancient kingdom, of blood feuds and cloak and dagger schemes in a land that seems to have sprouted on earth as nothing short of paradise.

Just consider some of its names. Fairy Meadows. Rama. Rupal. Kooto. Ultar. Gojal. Back in the States, I had browsed through some articles in travel magazines, enlarged a few pictures on the internet. The names alone held me captivate. Hunza. Gulmit. Rakaposhi. Nanga Parbat. And here I am, transporting myself to this otherworldly place among real life kings and queens.

"Who wants to change the music?"

A chorus of groans emerges from the back of the van.

"You had your turn. Now let us grownups enjoy some tunes."

The prince with the binoculars hands the driver a tape. Bollywood pop songs give way to Urdu *ghazals*.

"Ahh. This is more like it."

The prince leans back in his seat as the lilting voice of Noor Jehan wafts from the stereo. He closes his eyes and hums along some bars of the classic *Dil ke Afsane*.

I like the way the prince's wife is cradling her head in her husband's lap. She looks up at him and smiles as he slowly strokes her frizzy black curls. The couple is sitting across the aisle from me in the second row. In front of us sits the prince's mother, her eldest daughter-in-law and her two twin girls. Another daughter-in-law and daughter team, a couple of uncles and a batch of cousins occupy the rows further back. The driver is a family friend who is trading gossip with Adam, the only royal whose name I have managed to remember, for it is Adam who will be my travel companion/ chaperone/translator/ trekking guide for the next few weeks. He is all of nineteen years old and a complete mystery.

I had met Adam when I was invited to his parents' house for dinner. I had flown from Karachi back to Islamabad the night before. Adam had pretty much ignored me all evening. He didn't even say hello and kept leaving the dinner table at abrupt intervals without any explanation. Adam's father was much more personable. As managing director at PTDC, the Pakistani Tourism Development Corporation headquartered in Islamabad, Saeed Anwar Khan was keen to talk about the ins and outs of traveling within the country. He held up a hand and told me to call him Saeed, every time I referred to him as Mr. Khan. What really made us bond is when Saeed talked about his visits to Seattle and recalled his favorite hikes around Mount Rainier. The Carbon River Glacier. Mystic Lake. The Wonderland Trail.

It thrilled me to hear these familiar names from his lips. When Adam's father mentioned Snoqualmie Falls, I nearly fell from my chair, so unsettling it was to hear him voice my backyard haunts. Adam's mother, who was sitting with us smoking a clove cigarette from an elaborate silver holder, had to reach out and grab me by the arm to prevent me from tipping over. It was most inappropriate behavior, in front of the *Rani,* who had been a most gracious hostess. I learned that the departed Mir, Shaukat Khan, was her father who had been the ruler of the formerly princely state of Nagar. He was eighty six years old and survived by five other siblings, three sons and two daughters.

As far as first impressions go, Adam Khan could have used some pointers. He was a gangly teenager mostly preoccupied with the stubble on his chin and his chewed up fingernails. Limpid green eyes flickered in my direction every once in a while. Sometimes, he would fix his gaze at my feet and I suddenly became aware of how open and naked they appeared in my *kolhapuri* sandals. I wanted to say something to Adam to break the ice, but then he got up again and left the room.

It was not a promising start. Nonetheless, here I was on the cusp of a once in a lifetime road trip. Major Malik had mapped out an itinerary that I was free to improvise. He was especially keen on Chalt, the Mir's ancestral village. According to the Major, it was not to be missed. Chalt. Chalt. The name burrowed into my head.

The plan was for Adam and me to proceed north to Hunza to begin our mountain treks. The Major wanted us to get as far as the Pakistani-Chinese border at Khunjerab Pass with an elevation point of sixteen thousand feet. It all sounded so surreal, like something out of a Hollywood script. And in true movie making style, Adam and his crew showed up four days later at Aunty's place where I was taking refuge for a few days. It was a sunny morning in late July, perfect weather for a road trip in what appeared to be a Pakistani style trailer, an enormous oblong thing that looked rather like an oil tanker. My roommates looked outside and erupted into giggles.

I remembered the Major's parting words. "You've got the bug now. There's no going back."

*   *   *

We are traveling from Islamabad to Gilgit along the famed Karakoram Highway or KKH, one of the world's highest paved roads and informally known as the eighth wonder of the world. Connecting Pakistan to China, the narrow two-lane highway twists around three great mountain ranges and follows a swath of the ancient Silk Road where caravans of silks, spices, silver, gold, ivory crisscrossed east-west as early as the fourth century. Even without history, scenery, and wildlife, the Karakoram Highway would be noteworthy as an engineering marvel. Imagine a penknife trying to hack a passageway through a wall of granite for over nine hundred miles.

In 1966, the Pakistanis and Chinese began the challenge of building paved asphalt amidst a mountainous collision belt. They dubbed it the friendship highway. The entire project on Pakistan's side was entrusted to Army engineers with a semi-autonomous body, the Frontier Works Organization, (FWO) executing the roadwork. I had read a harrowing account of the project's initial phase as described by a Pakistani Army engineer.

> It took us two weeks to cover thirty kilometers. There was no suitable equipment. The supply of explosives was erratic and when snow blocked the Shangrila Pass, the

troops survived on local maize. There was no road to
follow, not even the semblance of one. Just a narrow
footpath that even donkeys found difficult to negotiate.
All supplies, including explosives, had to be carried by the
soldiers themselves on their backs. Most of the equipment
had to be dismantled and then carried to the next camp, to
be reassembled there. These were days of extreme hardship.

The Karakoram Highway was formally inaugurated and opened to road traffic in August of 1982, two months after I left Pakistan for America. The human cost of construction killed over eight hundred Pakistanis and roughly eighty two Chinese (the unofficial death toll is somewhat higher, amounting to nearly one life for each kilometer of road). According to some accounts, workers used to hang from helicopters to blast mountainsides with dynamite.

Our trailer cruises past Taxilla, once a Buddhist colony and the kingdom of the Hindu king Ashoka. After Abottabad, the Karakoram Highway starts climbing higher into the mountains. Saw tooth wedges interlock earth and sky while, far below, the Indus River churns its way south like a wriggling grey serpent returning the mountains to the Indian Ocean. The mouth of the Indus empties into the Arabian Sea where I used to go beachcombing as a child. Now I'm following its course upriver for the next three hundred miles paralleling the KKH which is lauded on one Pakistani tourism brochure as "the most brilliant achievement of mankind of the 20th century."

Karakoram is a Turkic term for crumbling rock. Landslides are a constant hazard. Heavy rains and flooding are common during monsoon season from July till August. We are lucky to have the weather on our side. But just in case it gets nasty, I'm told that bulldozer drivers from the Pakistani army are permanently deployed to deal with Mother Nature.

We appear to be riding a shelf carved into a sheer cliff face. A Suzuki truck passes us on the left. At least a dozen men are hanging off the rear fender and the sides. They stand upright clinging to dear life as their earth toned *shalwar kameez* outfits flutter in the breeze. The men's faces are wrapped in thick woolen shawls. Our driver revs up the engine eager to keep up with the passing vehicle, but it zips ahead already swallowed by the highway's curves. Every now and then, the road cuts a notch between sheer rock face below and the overhanging rock face above it, an open invitation to avalanches and mudslides. Massive angular mountains frame the skyline. Their grandeur turns Mount Rainier into an ant hill.

As the Karakoram highway reaches the tribal region of Kohistan, the Indus gouges a deep canyon between the walls of surrounding mountains and thrashes about in its confinement. Road workers in blue cotton jumpsuits and plastic helmets are using axes to break chunks of rock into smaller stones. Waterfalls of melting snow, moraine fields, and the drama of the river gorge compete for my attention as I try in vain to concentrate on one vista before something else distracts and compels me to absorb its magnificence. One of the royal members of our traveling troupe taps me on the shoulder to take back his binoculars. I regret not bringing along a video camera.

Across the aisle, the prince, who has taken over as DJ, continues humming to *ghazals*. I dub him humming prince. The tween section at the back of the bus is suspiciously silent. When I turn around to investigate, I see brothers, sisters, and cousins all head phoned to their portable Discmans. Adam is absorbed in a hand held video game. Humming prince flashes me a quick smile and takes his turn to recline in the wife's lap. Excitement pounds my nerves as I wonder what's in store in the Northern Areas.

"Internal Occupation," Major Malik had said when we discussed the region's history. "Ironic, don't you think, to link the oppression of one people to rationalize the denial of justice to your own population?"

According to the Major's explanation, as the British prepared to leave India and the creation of Pakistan was more or less imminent, the departing viceroy, Lord Mountbatten, handed the Northern territories to Maharaja Hari Singh of Jammu and Kashmir, who soon after acceded to India. Consequently, the people of Gilgit-Baltistan revolted and led an armed struggle against the Maharaja's decision. A ceasefire was announced on January 1st, 1949 whereupon the Northern Areas became a territorial part of Pakistan, but when it came to governance, the Northern Areas, unlike Pakistan's four other provinces, had no formal provincial status and no clear mention of basic political, legal and civil rights in the constitution.

There was a deliberate reason for this ambiguous policy and it was rooted in Pakistan's long standing conflict with India over Kashmir. According to the twisted logic of Pakistani governance, it was essential to maintain the semi-autonomous status of the Northern Areas which essentially denied the region both sovereignty and national integration. As a result, the Northern Areas were part of disputed territory, the same as Kashmir. How and why this worked in Pakistan's favor was a matter of simple mathematics. Two disputed territories would equal a larger vote bank should and if elections, instead of bombs, decide the outcome of Kashmir in the near future. Meanwhile, Pakistan was resigned to hold its own population hostage as human bargaining chips, irrespective of the blatant disregard of fundamental human rights and democratic norms.

I was surprised to hear this condemnation. Here at last was an internal critique of governance and politics from within the establishment fueled by Major Malik's passion for this little known and neglected part of Pakistan. When I asked the Major how long this internal siege mentality would last, he shrugged and referred to history. During the early 1900's, the Northern Areas, then part of British India, became the battleground for territorial dominance between the Brits and Czarist Russia.

The Major talked about Godfried Wilhelm Lietner, a linguist who wanted to learn Darri, one of the local languages. He came to explore the region and went back to warn the British about the dangers of a Russian attack through the mountain passes. Just the thought of being attacked by the Russian army, possibly aided by wild mountain tribes which could in turn lead to a revolt in the princely state of Kashmir and the whole of Northern India was enough to stir the Brits into action. They established a "forward policy" and set up a political agency in Gilgit and Chitral to keep closer tabs.

The Major picked out a paperback from his bookcase entitled *The Gilgit Game* and handed it to me.

"And what a mosaic of cultural, ethnic and linguistic groups!" he exalted. "Shina, Balti, Burushaski, Wakhi, Khuwar and Khilcha, these are some of the regional dialects. But they understand Urdu so you should be fine."

We were on our third cup of chai and I was already seduced. By sample day trips, hand drawn trail maps and more beguiling names. Dardistan. Baltistan. Bolaristan. Balwaristan.

"All historical references," the Major had said, "Of course, before forty-seven, there was no mention of the Northern Areas. But that's no excuse to leave the place in political limbo for over fifty years."

Besham is our overnight rest stop. I share a hotel room with the princess of Hunza, her androgynous twin daughters and the stately grandmother who was once a queen. She motions me to take the bed as she settles down on the floor and spreads out her shawl. I keep protesting, but she refuses to listen, her bony arms clutching my shoulder blades and positioning me firmly on the bed.

"It is alright," says her daughter. "My mother likes sleeping on the floor."

"But she would be so much more comfortable up here," I reply feeling utterly ridiculous.

The princess smiles and adds, "It is best this way. She does not mind."

Her mother smiles in my direction and the discussion is closed. The Hunza princess asks me to help unzip her *kurta*. Her skin is alabaster smooth and extremely fair. She shares the same light-skinned texture, pale green eyes and honey colored hair with her daughters. Conqueror's blood they call it and inform me of their genetic lineage to five wandering soldiers of Alexander the Great.

I rise early the next morning to say my dawn prayers and find the princess prostrating on a rug, a black chador draped over her head and shoulders.

"*Ashadoallah, la illaha illahu.*"

She raises her right index finger.

"*Asalamo rahmatullahi wa barkatahu.*"

She turns her head towards the right shoulder and then her left.

I join the princess and together we pray, rising and sitting in the same motions. The fact that she is a Shia and I'm a Sunni makes no difference. In this brief instance, we are the same before God.

Across the balcony, morning sunlight drenches the Indus in shimmering waves. I keep my shawl wrapped over my head as I had done for prayers and step outside to drink scalding hot tea from a thermos somebody has thoughtfully prepared. From a distance, the highway looks like a serrated incision carved into the mountain's belly.

*   *   *

Day two on the road reveals a changing landscape. The KKH enters a flatter terrain, dry and desert like with massive fields of boulders burnished brown like copper and bronze. The boulder field continues until Chilas, where roadside bandits are not uncommon. The Major had warned me to spend minimal time in Chilas, but the royal family elects to stop in town for lunch.

My encounter with danger is not the local dacoits, but the local water. The hotel waiter wobbles his head from side to side and ensures me the Nestlé water bottles contain pure spring water, but the parasites cramping my stomach soon dismantle his lie. Adam admonishes me for not being more careful.

"But how was I to know?" I fume. "It said Nestlé on the bottle so I assumed it was safe."

"Never assume anything in Pakistan," he says. "This is not your spic and span Amreeka. Here you have to watch your back all the time or else they will always get the better of you. If you must drink bottled water, make sure you break the seal from the bottle yourself."

"I know, I know. I just forgot."

It needn't have happened. I had been warned about drinking contaminated tap water allegedly made safe in plastic bottles with fake labels that were sold in the bazaar. It was a mean trick. I clutch my aching stomach and mull over the spic and span bit.

After lunch, Adam and I head to the hotel lobby and spread out my guidebooks and maps on the floor to work out a trekking itinerary, with Gilgit as our base. We don't make much progress, thanks in part to an impromptu advisory committee of various uncles gathered around us in a tight circle, offering suggestions, but really just trying to outdo each other's ideas.

Uncle #1: They should start at Naltar. The Switzerland of Pakistan!

Uncle #2: No no, you've got it all wrong. They should proceed straight to Rakaposhi. If you're fit enough, you should be able to climb up to base camp and make your descent towards the Hunza side. When you make it to Hunza, watch out for the tourist touts! They'll loot you for every rupee if you're not careful. Of course, one doesn't find too many tourists nowadays. The whole valley is deserted thanks to the Fundos. They've driven away all the foreigners

Uncle #3: Nonsense! My friends from Germany are on their way. Destination, Gojal, Upper Hunza. From there you can take in some of the biggest glaciers in the world. Hoper is my favorite. Most impressive.

Impressive indeed, but I am too confused to utter a word. Maybe it would have been better after all to have gone on a packaged tour and be spared the headache of figuring out what to see and how to see it. I am also worried about Adam. He is my designated travel companion, chaperone and guide for the next ten days, but we have yet to establish some rapport. I don't expect us to become instant friends, but a show of some enthusiasm on his part, a conversation or two that's not just a flurry of do's and don'ts would be most reassuring. Throughout the road trip, Adam has been deliberately avoiding me, sitting all the way in the back of the van, gossiping and giggling with the cousins, slipping on his headphones whenever I walked by.

Even last night at Besham, when we had all gathered for dinner in the gardens overlooking the river, Adam had chosen to sit on the far end of the table, leaving me ensnared between his mother and the Princess of Hunza, both of whom I liked very much, the mother especially, who had offered me her clove cigarettes and complimented my Kashmiri shawl. Back in our room, when she heard me tossing and turning in bed, Adam's mother had spoken in a firm and gentle voice.

"You will be in good hands. My son has his moods, but he knows how to take care of our guests. He will try to push you around at first, but that is his nature. He likes to test people before he takes them into his confidence. Don't let that worry you too much. My son has a heart of gold. He will be a like a brother to you if you learn to trust him. And if you need anything at all, if you get tired from all your walking, you are always welcome at the palace."

I took her words as a blessing of sorts. But my doubts hadn't dissipated. What did she mean by Adam's test and what kind of a test would I be subject to? And why was trust so important? I wasn't planning on marrying the boy. I just needed a reliable and knowledgeable guide. And if he really was the regional mountain expert his family raved about, then I had nothing to be concerned about. We would get along just fine.

"Go and sit next to the driver. You're missing out on all the fun with your face buried in that book. Here, give me that thing."

Humming prince reaches across the aisle and grabs my Lonely Planet trekking bible. He glances at the front cover and chuckles.

"You don't need this mumbo jumbo," he says. "Just feast your eyes on that!"

There are mule tracks etched along the mountainsides. They look like a modern art sketch of twisty spaghetti strands. The road weaves in and out of mountain flanks. In some parts, it narrows so much that there seems to be no room for two oncoming trucks or buses, but we manage to squeeze through amid a symphony of horns, whistles and cheers from passing vehicles.

I am now enjoying unobstructed views of the landscape having moved up front in the passenger seat. The driver points out more perilous etchings on the mountainside and then he tells me that before the KKH was built, the mule tracks were the only way of getting around the gorges. When the rock face became too sheer, the tracks would be replaced by rope ladders and when they were missing, the hapless traveler would have to jump down and land on a slim ledge to pick up the trail with the risk of a missed foothold plunging him into the churning river some eight hundred meters below. The driver makes a whooshing sound and laughs. All of a sudden, he clutches my sleeve and points to a massive slab of jagged rock protruding into the clear blue sky.

"Nanga Parbat."

It means naked mountain. A craggy toothed monster glistening in sun drenched snow. It is the eighth highest peak in the world, rising nearly twenty three thousand feet tall. According to local lore, Nanga Parbat's summit crowns a crystal kingdom of fairy spirits and mythical creatures. *Nanga Parbat.* I slowly repeat the name, enjoying the soft cadences of its Urdu syllables.

As we approach Gilgit, the highway abandons its curves as if slapped by a ruler to straighten up and behave. A taut ribbon of asphalt stretches into town. We arrive by sundown. Adam and I exit near a traffic roundabout leaving the royals on board to carry on to their destinations. Everyone waves goodbyes. I am not sure if I will ever see them again.

*   *   *

The Serena Lodge is one of Gilgit's poshest hotels. All slick and shine, it's hardly in line with my idea of roughing it in the great outdoors. But I give in to Adam's insistence that we splurge for one night, we meaning me, according to the terms of our travel arrangement where I am paying for accommodations and transport. To stretch my modest budget, Adam has checked us both in the same room. I don't really mind since Adam has amply demonstrated that he's not the least bit fascinated in me as a person of interest, let alone a woman, but I can't be sure how well our room sharing arrangement goes down with the hotel staff nor can I be bothered with their opinions and smirks.

"They will always take you for being loose," a friend in Boston had warned. "You're from America and a woman traveling by yourself in Pakistan. End of story."

I hang out in the lobby with the hotel manager. He orders two salty *lassis*, gestures grandly towards the patio terrace and talks in a sing song voice.

"You take drink with me. No worry, no worry. Your friend at pharmacy. Buy medicine for your tummy."

Thanks a lot Adam. I am famous already. Single woman. Aching tummy. Teenage escort.

I down the *lassi* in a single gulp and retire to my room. The sluggishness from the two day road trip and the parasites pinching my insides are not helping. Adam doesn't return until half past midnight, only to keep me awake with rustling plastic bags and numerous toilet flushes. He lies on the single twin bed on my left and moans in his sleep.

The following morning, a waiter motions me over to a table set with hot buttered toast and chai, which I have not ordered, but I manage to take a few nibbles and sip the tea which is overly sweet and lukewarm. I ask for some orange juice instead and watch the comings and goings in the lobby. A foreign couple is checking in. I can tell right away that they're not American because they're traveling far too light without any fancy gear. They look European, French or German most likely or maybe Austrian. Yes, why not. Go Austrians. I love Austrians.

The couple head out the lobby arguing about something. My mind flashes back to the Italian Dolomites. I had been hiking there solo three years ago enthralled with the rush of pure freedom as I trudged from one mountain hut to another and then one day the thrill ended when I got lost and found myself scrambling up a moraine field in the middle of nowhere. I heard some people shouting and waving their trekking poles in my direction. They turned out to be a friendly quartet of cousins from Vienna and adopted me into their circle, sharing their food and company and not letting me out of their sight until we had crossed over the mountain pass to Cortina from where I caught a train back to Rome. It had been a grand adventure, the kind that makes you wonder later on if you had dreamed it all up.

I'm hoping that I'll experience something equally adventurous and grand in the mountains of Pakistan, but it's so different here, not just in terms of terrain, but also the logistics of teaming up with a temperamental teenage guide who happens to be a prince.

They are out of fresh toast but there is *aloo ghosht* (meat and potatoes) or *palak paneer* (spinach with homemade cheese) on today's lunch menu. The manager comes up to say something about a driver waiting. I look out a side window and see a thin orange haired man polishing the fenders of a sea green jeep. He waves to me and calls me Madam. Apparently, Adam Khan has made all the travel arrangement and simply forgotten to show up. It is not until three in the afternoon that he saunters into the lobby where I am sitting cross legged playing Scrabble with the ever attentive manager. He gets a triple word score and claps his hands like a child. Adam lobs a grin.

"*Sahib e Alam!* How good of you to join us."

The manager rises on his feet and salaams the prince in an old fashioned, exaggerated style, sweeping his right hand from toe to forehead and walking backwards. He calls for more chai. It looks like we won't be budging from this place. I might as well camp out in the hotel, pitch my tent on the marble floor and eat granola for dinner.

"Relax," Adam tells me when I grumble about his tardiness. "We'll make it to Naltar in time."

I remember his mother's advice about trust. Adam knows best.

"Do you want some lunch?" I ask in my best UN Security Council negotiating voice.

"I'm not hungry," Adam replies. "I can get something later on the road."

Yay. He said it at last. Let's hit the road, Buster, Mister, Hustler. Highness. Huzoor. Whatever you are.

Adam digs into his pants pocket and fishes out a small bottle of pills that he tosses into my lap.

"For your tummy."

"Hurry up!" I shout. "We've already lost half the day."

"*Memsahib!*"

Adam motions towards the door. I grab my duffle bag with lightening speed and wave goodbye to the hotel manager who is standing nearby, still smiling and nodding ever so profusely.

"Goodbye, goodbye!" he says. "*Allah Hafiz.*"

God be with you. I certainly hope so.

The driver turns out to be a Hunza man. Adam slaps him on the back and opens a brand new pack of Gold Leaf. The driver takes two and tucks one cigarette behind the ear.

"We are technically enemies," Adam says. "He is from the other side of the river. The side that butchered my ancestors."

The driver grins and exposes a row of yellowing teeth. He tells me not to believe a word of what any Nagari says. They are cold, unfeeling people living on the dark side of the valley. The Hunzakuts face south towards the warming sun. That's why his people are more warm hearted and friendlier.

"Don't listen to him," Adam retorts. "He comes from a line of thieves and murderers!"

We scramble into the jeep where Adam has already stowed away his luggage. From Gilgit, it takes us about an hour to reach the village of Nomal, the closest village to the woodsy, alpine valley of Naltar, reputed as the Switzerland of Pakistan. Something appears to be wrong. There are policeman everywhere crisscrossing the road and waving their hands directing traffic to come to a standstill. The driver rolls down his window and makes a few inquiries. His Urdu is hard to understand, but we gather that access to Naltar is temporarily closed due to a robbery incident. The police are searching for the runaway thief and no vehicles are allowed to access the gravelly river road that leads into the valley.

We turn back and stop at Golden Peak Tours to regroup. It is managed by Liaqat, a lanky mild mannered cousin of Adam's with twinkling hazel eyes. The eyes appraise me and linger on my shawl covered breasts.

"You go straight to Karimabad in Hunza and see Naltar on the way back," Liaqat says.

I show him my hand written itinerary.

"Fine, fine. It is all possible. You get the car and driver for ten days. Go where you like. Adam Khan knows the area well."

And just like that, we hit the road towards paradise.

7

HUNZA HIGH

Karakoram Highway, August 2003

"AAYISTA, AAYISTA," Adam admonishes the driver to slow down.

He stops at the roadside where children are carrying baskets of fruit. They are selling fresh ripe apricots straight from the orchards sprawled throughout the valleys and villages along the highway. I buy a kilo's worth from one little boy and soon another boy approaches and then another and another. One enterprising girl holds out her palm filled with small red pellets that according to Adam are unpolished garnet. She empties the whole lot in my purse and refuses to take any money.

"Shukria."

I thank her and offer a packet of Trident chewing gum and a Hello Kitty pencil as a token of gratitude. She grabs them and dashes off to join the other kids who make a beeline in my direction as though I am Santa Claus.

It is a gorgeous day and we appear to be in a fairy tale land. Clear blue skies, velvety green fields, wildflower meadows, waterfalls gushing down mountainsides, and an amphitheater of snowy peaks towering all around. Photo ops beckon in every direction. I take some pictures of the children against the panoramic backdrop. They are uncomfortable in front of the camera and pose like statues with steely expressions. I urge them to loosen up and engage them in a game of tag in a nearby field. Just when it's my turn to be It, Adam starts honking like a madman. I wave goodbye to the kids and hurry back to the waiting jeep with my plastic sacks jiggling with apricots.

"What's the rush?" I ask. "We have all day to get to Karimabad."

Adam looks the other way and fumbles with the tape deck. He seems to take enormous pleasure in getting me all worked up. Peeved about the interrupted photo shoot, I sulk in the back seat wishing I could somehow get back at Adam for raising my blood pressure and spoiling my mood. The driver throws me a sympathetic look and says something about an urgent appointment that the prince must keep. It sounds rather sinister and when I glance towards Adam, he gives me that same blank stare that has been getting on my nerves ever since we left Islamabad. I try not to worry too much about what lies ahead and munch on the apricots as the driver merges onto the KKH.

We have been heading north for about three hours stopping every now and then for bathroom breaks and Adam's cigarette cravings. He keeps chain smoking and running out of his Gold Leaf packets and I wonder time and again how he can climb mountains while puffing away like a volcano. Adam has been unusually quiet since we turned back from Naltar. We had argued pretty viciously at his cousin's office about where we should go and which hikes to tackle and whether or not I was fit enough to handle the Northern Areas terrain which Adam insisted was not for amateurs whose idea of a strenuous stroll was confined to cruising around the local mall and that was enough to short circuit my temper and I practically lunged at the kid to yank his hair from the roots, just before Liaqat intervened, calming me down with a 7-Up and handing Adam an entire carton of Marlboros.

The cousin was a good mediator who had recognized early on that Adam and I were no better than a pair of tiresome toddlers bent on having their own way. Upon Liaqat's suggestion, we agreed to meet halfway by not enforcing an iron clad itinerary and breaking down the trip into three main sections, Hunza, Gulmit, Nagar. That would still leave us plenty of leeway for impromptu treks and day long hikes depending on my stomach bugs which were still healing and Adam's moods, which according to his cousin, were stable for the most part, until something or someone really agitated him and then you just never knew what you were in for. If that was supposed to make me feel better, I'm not sure that it worked, but having come so far, I had no choice but to simply make a go of it and surrender to the journey.

"Rakaposhi!" says the driver.

He points ahead and I find myself staring at a jagged hulk of ice and snow getting closer and closer. It is a stupendous mountain rising in an unobstructed full sweep that gets all the more commanding by the time we stop for a bite to eat at Rakaposhi View Point. It's a roadside shack jazzed up to look like a bohemian café. No one is there and our presence elicits an enthusiastic welcome from the middle aged owner who immediately lines up some plastic chairs and offers us tea. He talks with longing about the good old days when this place was routinely packed with foreign tourists. British. French. German. Japanese. American. There hasn't been much business after 9/11, except for the occasional locals from Karachi or Islamabad, mostly rich Pakistani kids who come with their friends and throw their weight about as though they own everything in sight. The foreigners were far more polite and generous in their tips.

Feeling rather hungry, I order an omelet. It's soggy and greasy, but I devour it just the same as Adam looks on with a smirk. He watches me as I square up the bill. I know he's trying to get something on me, to find some fault or mistake to laugh about. I don't know why the boy is so critical and I'm even more baffled as to why I care so much what he says or thinks about me.

"Let's go for a walk," I suggest.

Adam shrugs and I take it as a yes. We cross the road and set off on our first official hike just going up the grassy meadow at the base of Rakaposhi. It is steeper than it looks and I go too fast too soon. An hour later, I'm barely moving and breathing heavily. Adam is yards ahead of me despite all his nicotine breaks. I finally make it to the rock where he's reclining and blowing smoke circles at the sky. The prince lobs a sweet little smile that jabs me straight where it's meant to and I make a mental note never again to question his trekking skills or his smokes. Maybe there's some magic ingredient in those cigarettes that enable him to fly up the mountain slopes.

"It's getting late," says Adam. "We should try to be in Karimabad by nightfall."

He looks at me with his trademark poker face as though I have forgotten about his mysterious rendezvous. It's either a drug dealer or a girlfriend. I bank on the latter and try to suppress the urge to laugh out loud.

"Sounds like a plan," I reply. "Do they have a pharmacy there? I'm going to need more antibiotics again. My stomach is still acting up."

"Don't worry about it. You worry too much. That's your whole problem. Just like an American. They're all worry warts."

He could have skipped the lecture, but I don't feel like arguing. Our impromptu trek has lightened my mood. I'm up for anything now.

"OK. I won't worry. Happy now?"

Adam smiles.

"We'll get you everything you need."

* * *

Fabled Hunza was not always so easily reached, nor so tranquil. In older days, pilgrims, traders and imperial invaders had to navigate the area on narrow foot trails penciled along the valley walls. "Noisy with kingdoms" was Marco Polo's take on Hunza in the year 1273. During the 1960s and 70s, the people of Hunza briefly became famous in the West for harboring the fountain of youth, supposedly living to over a hundred years of age, sustained by pure high altitude mountain air and an equally pure vegetarian diet rich in almonds, apples, cherries and apricots. This made an impression on an eccentric American optometrist by the name of Allen Banik who traveled to Hunza in 1958. He was sent there by Art Linkletter, a Hollywood TV personality who hosted a show called *People are Funny*. Hollywood must have been an enlightened place in those days. Mr. Linkletter encouraged Dr. Allen Banik to discover the Pakistani Shangri-la and bring back its secrets.

In his travelogue *Hunza Land,* Banik writes one glowing account after another such as:

The men in Hunza have broad shoulders and slim waists. Their walk is a smooth effortless glide. Their ruddy features have the hardy endurance of mountain folk who don't appear to know the meaning of fatigue.

Karimabad, the largest settlement in Hunza, inhabits one of the most benign vales of the Himalayan-Karakoram chain. Lush orchards laden with fruit and fields corduroyed with rows of crops glow in the late afternoon sun. Stepped terraces wrap around ingenious irrigation channels that over the centuries have transformed this harsh mountain terrain into Pakistan's breadbasket. As we follow the road into the capital of Hunza Valley, Adam points out a gnarled walnut tree that is supposedly five hundred years old. We proceed to a budget inn after I turn down Adam's offer to stay at the Mir's refurbished palace hotel.

"I could have gotten us a good deal," he protests. "They are my family after all."

All well and good, but luxury accommodations are the farthest thing from my mind when I am still sick with the parasites and feeling slightly feverish. This is no time for swirling champagne with royalty. Or even Hunza water, the locally made mulberry wine that was surely the secret of their longevity.

By dinner time, my stomach cramps are becoming unbearable. Adam takes off in search of a pharmacy to get me more medicine which doesn't seem to be working. I crawl into bed and curse the stupid waiter from Chilas. Damn that waiter and his tap water bottle. Why did I have to touch it? Why couldn't I just follow directions or learn to suspect everything in Pakistan? Why do I have to be so gullible and naïve? Adam knocks on the door and brings me a plate of plain boiled rice and Seven-Up. He tells me not to wait up as he's going out with a friend. I don't bother to ask who or where.

"Don't look so sad," Adam says. He sits beside me in bed and strokes my hair. "You will be alright in a few days. If not, we will go see a Doctor. We have good hospitals here. You are not in some *junglee* wilderness. So just relax."

He could really be charming if he wanted to. I lean my head on the prince's shoulder and spill some tears. It's turning out all wrong.

There will be no scenic treks amid glaciers and waterfalls, no lavish picnic lunches along riverside lodges, no back country camping in meadows bursting with color. The pictures in my head turn to mush. We may have to postpone the entire excursion and return to Gilgit.

"Relax, just relax," Adam croons.

I fall limp into the pillow as he switches off the bedside lamp and leaves the room. His parting words echo in my ears.

"Feel everything. Feel it deeply. Do everything with love. *Pyar aur mohabat se.*"

In the morning, we have company for breakfast. Iftikhar is an old friend of Adam's and a local merchant dealing in gemstones. He entertains us with century old yarns about courtly shenanigans when Hunza was still a princely kingdom. According to Iftikhar, the ruling Mir had a tendency for raiding the caravans that passed on their way from Central Asia to British India. When the English Captain Francis Younghusband confronted the Mir of Hunza in 1889, his royal highness had a ready answer. The caravans were his only source of income. But if it made Queen Victoria unhappy, he would be happy to cut her in on the booty. The Mir's diplomacy was not viewed favorably by Younghusband who sent in the British Army to better explain the imperial point of view.

There is hearty laughter all around and some rude remarks about the Brits.

"Clever old buggers," remarks Iftikhar.

"Bloodsuckers," says Adam.

"Long live the Union Jack!"

I wave an imaginary flag and help myself to more tea. Iftikhar hands me a business card and invites me to visit his shop in downtown Karimabad where I can get a special discount. Adam and I exchange a look, the first look of mutual understanding that we've shared since the start of our journey. He knows rightly that I have no intentions of visiting his friend's shop, that I only took the card and murmured something about being delighted out of politeness and that my real intent is to hit the road as soon as possible and get closer to the mountains. Maybe we can be friends after all, the prince and I.

He really was so sweet to me last night when I was feeling wretched and hopeless, and maybe that display of compassion was all I needed to make a speedy recovery. My stomach cramps are finally gone. Feeling like a new woman, I decide to spend a few hours exploring the town. It suits Adam just fine. He'll hang out with his relatives at the Mir's hotel and meet me by lunchtime at 1 PM. It's the first time we have agreed on a plan without any third party intervention or cigarette bribes. Adam offers a mock salute as he leaves the breakfast table. I almost blow him a kiss, but not wanting to attract any further attention from the waiters and guests, I simply wave.

Karimabad's winding main drag is lined with handicraft boutiques and a bookshop/cafe with a working espresso machine. My appetite has returned and I treat myself to chocolate cake and two cappuccinos while writing postcards and listening to the ambient songs of U2's *Joshua Tree* album. When I return to the hotel, Adam is waiting in the dining room and sipping chai with the driver.

"Did you see the fort?" Adam inquires.

"Fort? What fort?"

Adam sighs and rolls his eyes. "I should have known that you couldn't do a thing on your own without my assistance," he remarks. "What's the use of all those guidebooks you're lugging around if you can't even put them to any use!"

It's happening again. Just when I thought we had reached some sort of truce, he's treading on my nerves just to make his point. I won't let him get away with it.

"For your information, I had no intentions of visiting this fort, or whatever it is you're talking about. I've had a perfectly good time in a very nice bookstore. Look at what I bought!"

I show him my new collection of art books and travel guides as though I'm six years old again showcasing my Barbie dolls with color coordinated outfits.

Adam is not impressed. He cannot fathom my interest in books. Apparently, I'm the daftest tourist he's ever come across. No other Americans and Europeans he has catered to over all these years had missed the fort in Karimabad. There were actually two of them. Altit and Baltit. Adam prefers the Baltit, restored to its original glory with painstaking effort using advanced renovation techniques developed in Europe. He tells me the entire building which was built in the thirteenth century was taken apart stone by stone and reassembled with money from the Agha Khan Foundation. The fort also had some grand views of Rakaposhi and Hunza Valley. I was an idiot to have missed out on such a historic and beautiful place. All tourists go there. All tourists that is except for me.

Ignoring Adam's spiel, I absorb myself with the lunch menu and make a mental note of returning to the bookshop for one more espresso. It was a far bigger thrill than some dusty old forts.

We end the day by taking the jeep to Eagle's Nest, a viewpoint where four snowy peaks--Ultar, Rakaposhi, Lady Finger and Golden Peak--showcase their splendor like beauty queens vying for attention. The driver tells me that the Karakoram mountain range is considered in local folklore as the meeting point of heaven and hell. He speaks three languages, his native Burashaski, Urdu, and patchy English that he has picked up from tourists.

"Do you have place like this in your home in Amreeka?"

The driver sweeps his hand across the formidable mountains, their massive shadows shimmering and dancing in the dusky light. I imagine the Karakorams being karate-chopped by an angry God, the crumbling rocks glued back together somewhat haphazardly by benign fairies and elves that had paid attention to the esthetics of their labor resulting in this jagged frieze of granite with delicate Willow tree slopes and lush emerald terraces.

No, most certainly not. I had never seen such a place at home. In Amreeka.

*   *   *

It is not every day that one gets to sleep on a bed made out of solid gold. But then again, I wouldn't expect anything less at the Mir's palace.

We have finally made it to Nagar. The rival kingdom across the river from Hunza. One of the remotest of the Northern Area fiefdoms. And home to Adam and his family. It is well past sundown by the time we reach the palace, the journey along the five mile gravel track on the edge of a ravine with no margin of error, both terrifying and exhilarating. It had gotten downright death defying when Adam had taken over the jeep coaxing the driver to let him have a go at it by enticing him with two new packs of Gold Leaf. Then he put one of the cigarettes in his mouth and turned up the volume as the cassette rewound and we heard for the umpteenth time the beguiling lyrics of *Pahoron ki Kasam*. You cannot translate this song literally. You just have to feel it.

And what I felt every time was a combination of joy and melancholy, unrestrained and boundless. I loved the singer's throaty passion that sounded vaguely Pashtun or Afghan. Adam told me he was my namesake. Masood. Kamal Masood. Then Adam reached over to hand me the cassette cover from inside the glove compartment, almost losing control of the steering wheel and plunging us into the raging river.

"Lookout!" I had screamed. "Watch where you're going!"

Adam Khan remained calm.

"This is the life," he uttered. "All I need is a girl by my side." The prince glanced at my disheveled figure. "The right girl," he added mischievously.

"Welcome, welcome!"

I'm delighted to see that the whole gang is here. Royal aunties, uncles and cousins. Adam's mother and grandmother give me a warm welcome hug. Humming prince thumps me on the back and inquires about my parasites. He introduces me to his two slender teenage daughters who hadn't accompanied us on the road trip from Islamabad, but had instead flown into Gilgit on a twin engine Fokker plane that flew through cloudbanks to avoid hitting the mountain peaks. All the family members have gathered at the palace for a memorial service of sorts on the *chaliswah* or fortieth day of mourning following the death of the old Mir.

Visitors come and go offering their condolences. Everyone is busy talking, eating and mingling. There must be enough food to feed the whole village. I wander around the perimeter of the palace gardens, one side facing the cliff side dwellings of the villagers and the other overlooking a chainsaw ridge softened pink and lavender in the receding twilight. The palace itself is a sprawling stone bungalow with a modest simple design. I meet its principal residents, Prince Barkat, his vivacious Punjabi wife and their two daughters, Saima and Fouzia. They look me up and down and politely shake hands.

Dinner at the palace is a raucous affair. Men, women and children gather in big circles on the floor and help themselves to mountains of rice piled on top of huge silver platters. I sit with Prince Barkat, his wife and the Hunza mother and her daughters from the road trip. The identical twin girls are wearing tie dye T-shirts and bleached denims. They scrutinize my cotton *shalwar kameez* ensemble, the crumpled *dupatta* draped over my shoulders, as though I'm wearing a bunch of rags.

"Why are you dressed like that?" one of the sisters asks rather abruptly.

I mumble something about comfort, respect for the culture, and going incognito. The girls burst into laughter.

"Incognito? But you've got it all wrong! Do yourself a favor and stick to jeans and sneakers."

Maybe she had a point. It was true, the stares and smirks in public had followed my every move. I had learned to dismiss them, having accepted myself as the circus freak that comes to town. At least it was better than being a Nobody back home. Not having brought a single pair of jeans to Pakistan, my hiking attire consisted of baggy linen pants and a knee length *kurta* with my scarf wrapped around my head like a turban to keep off the sweat.

I recalled what had happened when Adam and I were trudging up the slopes of Rakaposhi. We ran into a group of Pakistani mountaineers, all geared up in sturdy boots, fleece and parkas. They were a serious looking bunch, marching single file, arms swinging back and forth like synchronized pendulums. As the men approached closer, they were having trouble looking straight ahead. One by one, their gazes shifted in my direction. Amusement gave way to plain old horror. I really should have brought some jeans.

"Is that all you're having?" The Hunza princess eyes my meager portions of yogurt and chapatti.

I tell her that I'm vegetarian, but the princess cannot fathom why on earth anyone would want to eat "rabbit foods" by choice. It doesn't go down well in a culture of mutton and kebabs. Not wishing to be sidelined by my eating habits, I change the subject and try to get the Prince's reaction to the dismal state of tourism in a region that heavily depends on tourist revenue as the backbone of its economy.

"A pity really," he says.

It was indeed. The news reports had blown it all out of proportion. Al-Qaeda was certainly alive and well but the Al-Qaeda threat to the traveler did not apply to Pakistan's remote Northern Areas. There was nothing here except absolute pristine mountain wilderness that not many people seemed to know about. And the ones who did know were too afraid to come. I hadn't realized how real the threat was perceived to be until I received an email from a climbing friend in Seattle, someone who had at one point, scaled the base camp of K2 and cycled down the Karakoram Highway. Now that same person was fearful of terrorists trampling over the Shangri-la he had once so revered.

Back in Karimabad, I had emailed my friend to tell him I had finally made it to the Northern Areas. He wrote back warning me to watch out for suspicious looking packages. It was no use convincing him otherwise.

Prince Barkat makes a perfect circle of meat and rice and pops it into his mouth. He chews contentedly and passes me a plate of cucumbers and radishes that's out of my reach.

"You're right," I say. "It's a shame to find the valleys so empty."

The prince goes on to add that the valleys are on sale. In an effort to boost tourism, the Pakistani Government has been advertising a blue light special. 50% reduction in climbing permits for peaks above six hundred and fifty meters, no charge for six hundred and fifty meters and below. Officials at the Pakistani Mountaineering Association and the Ministry of Tourism are hopeful that the slashed fees will attract more mountaineers like my friend from Seattle.

North Pakistan: Asia's Best Kept Secret is still the advertising slogan of Karakoram Jeep Treks International (KJTI). Never mind the guest houses with record vacancies. Mountain villages once teeming with foreign backpackers are now deserted amidst fears of violence and terrorist attacks. Thanks to Bin Laden, I am enjoying this earthly paradise all to myself.

By the time tea arrives, we have a newcomer in our circle, a burly gray haired man by the name of Salim whose credentials to the royals are largely based on his mother having been a wet nurse to one of the Mirs. When Salim hears that I'm from Seattle, he is eager to learn the whereabouts of a Mr. Jim Whittaker with whom he had climbed

K2 as his co-liaison officer in the 1978 expedition. Much to his disbelief, I tell him that I do not know Mr. Jim Whittaker personally. I only knew that he was the first American to have reached the summit of Mount Everest, back when Kennedy was President. Salim jots down his email address in case I can offer him further news of his old climbing buddy.

So it happens again. I am reminded of my Seattle connection in this far-flung Pakistani wilderness and I'm beginning to think that it's not so random. Is it just coincidence that Adam's father has hiked on the slopes of Mount Rainier? Is my meeting with Salim who knew Jim Whittaker largely accidental? It's almost as if I'm watching my two worlds, America and Pakistan, oscillating next to each other and I'm more and more uncertain as to which world I truly belong in.

After dinner, I venture into the palace gardens where they have lit a bonfire. There is no trace of Adam. He must be hobnobbing with his cousins, probably smoking a joint or two. A few yellow lights are visible across the palace, the only signs of life in the village on this star studded night. I return to my room and fall asleep on the golden bed reserved especially for me. The princess from Hunza is quietly snoring on the floor.

The next morning after breakfast, Prince Barkat takes out some old books and papers and shares some of his ancestral history. I learn that the Nagar royal family is part of the Mugholot Dynasty as descendents of Yaj the Third, a Persian king related to the Sassanians. The dynasty started when two princes fled from Iran to escape Arab rule. They came over the mountains and settled in what is now Skardu, the Baltistan region of Pakistan's Northern Areas and the area around Gilgit.

Many years down the line, there was a royal birth of Siamese twins. According to legend, a sword cut them apart and ever since then, the brothers became enemies for life. Since they could not stand to be near one another, they opted to live in opposite valleys separated by a river. The rivalry continued among their offspring in Hunza and Nagar though it did not prevent them from marrying one another in order to consolidate political power against foreign encroachers. Prince Barkat had diluted the royal bloodline by marrying an outsider, a Punjabi woman with Indian roots. His study is lined with books in

English, Urdu, Sanskrit and Persian. I admire an antique sword with an intricately carved jeweled handle. Prince Barkat tells me that it belonged to the Mughal emperor Jehangir.

I thank the prince for his hospitality and apologize for any inconvenience my presence may have caused.

"Not at all, my dear. Not at all," he says. "Come back to visit us anytime."

*   *   *

"Chalo, chalo!"

Let's go! Let's go!

Adam is getting impatient from waiting nearly two hours. I wave goodbye to Prince Barkat and his family and dash towards the palace gates where the jeep has its engine running.

"Wait, wait! I forgot my pack!"

Adam calls me *pagli,* crazy. I take it as a term of endearment.

Our commotion attracts attention and by now, the entire royal clan is outside watching our hasty departure. Somebody brings my pack and tosses it in the back seat. We get loads of food as though we're embarking on a desert expedition. It's more than generous and rather touching.

"Cheerio!"

"Bye!"

"Have a safe journey!"

I catch a glimpse of the widowed grandmother looking in my direction with her right hand over her heart. I do the same and keep my eyes fastened on her diminutive frame until she is no longer visible.

Back on the Karakoram Highway, the scenery gets more spectacular as we head in the direction of upper Hunza. The road rides high above a riverbank, twisting and turning around the barren foot of the Hispar Range where six of the peaks tower above twenty three thousand feet. On the opposite side, villages cling to mountainsides. What looks from a distance like piles of cigarette ash turns out to be grey rock and gravel slithering down into the river. As the highway crosses

Shishkot Bridge, we are surrounded on both sides by more saw-toothed ridges. The driver tells me that from here to China, the people speak a language known as Wakhi. Five miles past the bridge, we enter the village of Gulmit, a fertile plateau about eight thousand feet high, of lush green farmland on either side of the road.

Adam asks the driver to stop next to a small handicrafts shop. There is no compulsion to buy, but I am smitten with jade and lapis jewelry, hand embroidered throws, woolen jackets, caps and shawls. A man sitting next to a small charcoal brazier watches my excitement.

"You are my first customer in six months," he says.

Suleiman has one of those chiseled matinee idol faces that could never get tiresome. His piercing black eyes flicker with amusement as I poke around the dark, dingy corners of his shop searching for treasures.

"One moment," he says and disappears into a back room shortly returning with an armload of tapestries in muted earth tones. Then he brings out a magnificent headdress with a fringe of tiny mirrors and beads.

"Very old piece," he says. "From Tajikhistan."

I look into a mirror as Suleiman stands behind me and adjusts the headpiece so it rests flush against my forehead.

"That's better," he steps back and speaks to my reflection. "It suits you. Now you are like Tajik woman!"

I stare back at Suleiman and picture him in Armani gliding down a Milan catwalk. The photographers would go wild.

"Arre yaar, kuch chai wai to pesh karo!"

Adam comes into the shop demanding tea. I snap out of my reverie and place aside the headdress. I am not worthy of it, but I will take a half dozen cushion covers and a sable embroidered Hunza coat. Suleiman wraps the purchases in old newspapers and ties them with a piece of string. It seems futile to bargain. He doesn't even ask for the money, but discreetly slips a piece of paper scrawled with some numbers in my palm. The package has already been transferred to the back of the jeep. We are invited to not only tea, but to a homemade lunch of lentil soup, kebabs, and chapatti. A small boy brings over the meal in a stacked stainless steel *tiffin* box.

"From my wife." Suleiman explains. "Every day she is sending. Today she sends more for my guests! Please sit and enjoy."

Adam, I, and the driver recline on thick carpeted cushions and savor the food. Suleiman offers to get me some water, but I decline and stick to my own supply of Nestlé bottles without the fake seals. I tell him about the incident at Chilas.

"No one there is to be trusted," declares Suleiman. "They are all liars and thieves!"

For a man living in a remote mountain village in Northern Pakistan, Suleiman is astonishingly plugged into the world. After lunch, he shows me a stack of postcards from former customers. They bear stamps from Germany, France, Italy, Japan, Turkey and the US (New York). I particularly like one card from Iran. It features a close up of a turquoise glazed tile. Suleiman turns it over and reads aloud.

"My Dear Suleiman, I am writing to you from the world's most beautiful teahouse. It is in Shiraz. You remember Shiraz? You showed it to me on the map when we were sitting in your shop on that lovely summer's day. I hope you are happy. Your friend, Cathy."

"Who was she?" I ask.

"A very nice lady," he says. "From Canada."

"Do you still keep in touch with her?"

"I write her email. When I go to Gilgit for business, I stop at internet café."

How small the world gets with the click of a mouse.

"Will you give me your address?"

He jots it down in my notebook and makes an announcement.

"Tonight, you will have dinner with me. Brand new hotel. Very nice atmosphere. Good food. Good people. You will be my guests." Suleiman looks expectantly towards Adam and me.

It seems rude to say no. He will be hurt if we turn down his generosity. It is a question of honor and respect. *Izzat.* His *izzat* reflects ours.

"Thank you. It is most kind of you," I say.

Suleiman's charcoal thick brows arch defiantly in a gesture of approval.

"Very good! Very good!"

*   *   *

Gulmit makes for an ideal stopover, marking the halfway point between Gilgit and the Chinese border. It has already scored high marks in my book after meeting Suleiman. Adam tells me he is Ismaili, like most everyone in town. The Agha Khan, a spiritual leader of the Ismaili sect, funds the village schools and agricultural projects. Most of Hunza has been developed by the Agha Khan Rural Support Plan as indicated by the little green signs bearing the AKRSP logo posted near hospitals, clinics, schools and fields.

We pull into the driveway of a guesthouse that has the cozy look of a country estate. The owners of the Marco Polo Inn are distant relatives of Adam from the feuding Hunza side. They seem to be getting on rather well what with all the cheek kisses and slaps on the back. Adam lugs my pack and his duffle bag and puts them in two separate rooms that on closer inspection are stand alone cottages overlooking an orchard of apricot trees. There are no other guests staying and the manager lets us have free reign, insisting that we do away with formalities and treat the place as home.

I gravitate towards the open air verandah from where there is a ringside seat to Gulmit's star attraction, the Golden Peak of Karoun also known as Cathedral Spires. It's impossible to keep my eyes away from its commanding presence. Just like the scenery on the Karakoram Highway, describing something this spectacular stunts your speech.

You try to summon the words but they are just glossy adjectives. You have no choice but to string them together like beads and lasso it onto the object of affection which will forever outsmart your capacity to comprehend what you are seeing, for it is otherworldly and unknowable.

Since there is ample time before dinner, Adam wants to do some exploring. I grab my camera and wait for him in the jeep.

"Where's the driver?" I ask when Adam shows up with the keys.

"Gone."

"Gone? Gone where? We only just got here."

"Just try to relax and enjoy the ride," says Adam as he lights up a cigarette.

"I'm not going."

"Suit yourself."

"You're impossible!"

"Still not going?"

The engine is idling and I'm not budging from my seat.

"Whatever."

It soon becomes obvious that walking, rather than driving, would have been more efficient. Gulmit's layout is basically a vertical spiral of stone walled huts that wrap around terraced fields. The jeep struggles up the gravel bends. The valley is a quilt of green and yellow patches spiked with tall poplar trees. Women squat on their haunches winnowing grain. Instead of a veil, they are wearing little embroidered pill box hats that the older ones attach to a cotton chador.

I like how they wear their hair in long side plaits, that some of them wrap around in coils to resemble earmuffs. They use their hands like visors and stare at us as we wave. Adam juts out his chin and coaxes the jeep to keep on climbing. He has taken good care of me so far. But there is something about his manner that makes me uneasy. I'm not sure what it is exactly, perhaps the way he appears so poised and confident, rather too mature for his young age. His sense of self-assuredness makes me doubt mine.

The village children are skittish like young kittens. They scamper around us as we park the jeep under a shady tree. A teenage boy in a sky blue *shalwar kameez* offers to show us around. We walk through fields planted with bean crops. The high altitude air is sharp and clean. The boy regards me with a wary eye when I start taking pictures. He says something to Adam in a local dialect. Adam throws back his head and laughs.

"He is asking me if you are *jasous*. I think you are some kind of spy."

I choose to ignore Adam's comment and focus my attention on the village instead. It may be remote, but the boy is not shielded from the ways of the world. He knows about secret agents, which also leads me to believe that he knows about and possibly pines for a place where water comes from a faucet instead of a well, where there is a proper indoor bathroom and not an outhouse with a hole in the ground, where life in general is more comfortable and convenient. All this show stopping mountain beauty doesn't obscure the impoverished conditions these villagers have to endure.

It almost makes me feel foolish and decadent to come up here to take pretty shots of the indigenous culture and their quaint ways of living. I will arrange them in an album, throw in some nice captions and show them to friends back in the States who would say things like beautiful and adorable and stunning without truly comprehending the harsh, Spartan existence of an Alpine wonderland.

I'm well aware of the double standards involved. The way my privilege of living in the West sometimes makes me long for a Pakistan that is of another time, older, historical, and traditional. Authentic is the word I had used in Karachi when I couldn't wait to get out of the hurly burly whirl of the city and all its modern accoutrements. This village feels so pure and real. And if it were to lose its purity in the oncoming tide of globalization, a part of me would feel betrayed and disappointed to see the charming mud brick huts give way to concrete apartment blocks, the wholesome organic cuisine substituted by fast food outlets and the local kids fixated with their iPods and cell phones instead of gathering around a fire, singing folksongs and sharing stories and fables. It may never happen here in Gulmit, but the possibility alone makes for a hazy future. I'm not sure if I would want Gulmit to change much at all, only so far as allowing its residents to have some basic conveniences that I enjoy and sometimes take for granted. How much is enough is a delicate balance.

Adam and I are invited to meet the boy's father at his home. I shake hands with a tall, bony man with sunken cheekbones and graying hair. He calls me *beti* which means daughter. We sit on low carved wooden chairs and drink chai flavored with salt as they cannot afford sugar. The room is fairly large with an earthen floor, a flat tin roof, and walls with built in shelves that display cooking pots in gleaming aluminum. Only the ghetto blaster covered with an embroidered cloth fringed with beads seems slightly out of place. A frothing mountain stream gurgles outside the open front door.

Both father and son are composed and quiet. They don't ask a lot of nosy questions and their reserved manners are both unnerving and pleasing. We turn down their invitation to stay for dinner on account of our prior engagement with Suleiman and also because it would clearly stretch the modest means of our hosts. Their generosity is touching and I am reluctant to leave this dignified company for the razzle dazzle of city comforts in the valley below where Suleiman is waiting for us in the fancy hotel restaurant.

When we get there, it feels like another planet. The brocade fabric covered oversized menus with the fancy calligraphy appear silly and wasteful. I am in no moods for eggs Benedict or tuna cutlets with a dollop of house mayonnaise. Suleiman orders lamb *biryani* and urges me to try the grilled shrimp. I order stewed vegetables with plain rice because my stomach is starting to feel queasy again. The bottle of Nestle water at our table remains untouched. It's probably fine, but I'm in no mood to take any more chances. My thoughts are still occupied with the father and son duo. Despite all their hardships, I envy their simple lifestyle. Even if I had stayed and sampled their home cooked food, perhaps a soup made from potatoes and carrots, I wouldn't have really come close to understanding my hosts. The innate discipline and honesty of their lives was plain to see, but simply eating their food and sleeping on their floor was not enough to make me one with this humble pair. Our worlds were too far apart.

*   *   *

The next day, we climb into the jeep to take in some roadside glacier attractions. Just past Gulmit, the Gulkin Glacier snakes down low, practically licking the edge of the highway with its snout. A few yards ahead, we see the Passu Glacier in shiny white crinkles. Rising above it is a crystal lineup of peaks averaging twenty thousand feet. The driver points out a terrifying footbridge made out of twigs hung across the river, from where the valley fans out in a semi-circle of more serrated summits. Passu is a village of farmers and mountain guides about ten miles beyond Gulmit. Adam tells me it is the setting-off point for climbing expeditions and trekking trips up the Batura Glacier. Fifty seven kilometers in length, it ranks as one of the longest in the world.

We drive by the deserted Passu Inn which was once a burgeoning meeting place for travelers. Nearby is a road-side monument where a couplet by Dr. Muhammad Iqbal, Pakistan's philosopher-poet has been carved into the rock. The two lines are an appropriate tribute to the road-builders. Translated from the Urdu, the lines say:

When men set their minds to it, they can kick a mountain into powder.

The Karakoram Highway passes through four more villages before reaching the immigration and customs post at Sost. From here, China is less than a hundred kilometers, but we have decided not to proceed as far as Khunjerab Pass, even though the border has recently reopened after the SARS virus outbreak. I remember the Major's insistence to make it to Khunjerab, the world's highest international border crossing at nearly sixteen thousand feet. There is a point on the pass where one could step simultaneously on the soil of three countries--Pakistan, China and Tajikistan.

I should have thought this through when I planned my itinerary. It's silly to come this far and turn back, but I don't have much money left, certainly not enough to get us all the way to China. The driver makes a U-turn and we head back towards Gulmit. I'm not at all disappointed as Gulmit turns out to be my favorite place in Hunza. We spend the next three days exploring the valley.

One day, we walk down to the Hunza River where a scary suspension bridge beckons thrill seekers. It hangs high above the river and sways madly when Adam walks across its center. He doesn't seem to mind the missing planks exposing the torrential river below, but moves with ease as though he could do this blind folded. I don't dare take a step except to stand on the very first plank, ensuring my safety by hanging onto the iron cables supporting the structure.

Borit Lake turns out to be a bore. Apart from some mallards, there is nothing much of interest at the lake. We hang out for a while, but it's not all that enjoyable with Adam staring daggers at me without uttering a word of whatever is on his mind. I'm running out of patience and what's more, though I don't want to admit it, because of all the fuss I made about coming to this Pakistani Shangri-La, I'm starting to tire of the great outdoors. It is all starting to look the same. I can't tell the difference between a glacier and a stream nor do I seem to care.

A change of scene is definitely in order. I consider returning to Gilgit just in time to make the jeep caravan for the annual polo festival at Shandur Pass. There's a standing invitation from Adam's hazel eyed cousin, but Adam strongly discourages me from going.

"You won't like it," he declares. "It's a zoo up there. They call it culture, but it's really just a bunch of mad foreigners and rich Pakistanis partying all night. There's booze and sex and all kinds of crazy shit. I don't think it's your cup of tea."

It sounds like the local version of Burning Man at twelve thousand feet altitude. Rumor has it that the Prince of Wales, Charles himself, will be in attendance. The Shandur festival. That's where I should go next. Adam has a better idea.

"We'll go to Minapin and hike to Tagaphari. You will get to see Rakaposhi base camp. It's an awesome trek. All foreigners love it."

I may be tired of glaciers and streams, but I can't say no to Rakaposhi. So that's our plan. Good thinking Adam Khan. We go back to the Marco Polo inn, collect our bags and by five in the evening, we're pulling into the parking lot of the Diamer Hotel in a walled orchard near a mosque. It will be our base for the next three days, about as long as this eighteen kilometer walk will take us if we keep up a moderate pace. Adam insists it's not a technical climb. All I need is endurance and I seem to have plenty of it.

"How long will you stay in Pakistan?" Adam inquires.

"Don't really know. I'd still like to see more of the country. Definitely Peshawar again."

"Peshawar!" Adam scoffs. "Who wants to go to that hell hole?"

I'm disappointed that he doesn't share my fascination with Peshawar. Filthy old place filled with war mongering Pathans is Adam's take whenever the subject comes up. According to Adam, those guys only live for their guns and hashish.

It's understandable. He is a prince after all. You can't expect a prince to have much common ground with a group of men who are at best self described freedom fighters seeking justice and equality, at worst tribal militias and power crazed law givers destroying the very structure of their society. The one thing Adam has in common with them is his loathing for the West, namely the United States which he characterized time and again as a sick society. Often times, I was perceived as one of the sickoes with my only trump card being my Pakistani birth which in Adam's eyes didn't count for much as I had been away from the country for so long.

I gave up reasoning with him when he refused to see me as a practitioner of both cultures, East and West, Pakistan and America.

And it puzzled me for the longest time, why despite all his resentment, Adam Khan would never be the sort to pilot airplanes through buildings even though he admired the dare devil attitude and sheer madness it took to perpetrate the 9/11 attacks.

When I had jokingly suggested that Adam should venture to Afghanistan to wage war against the sickened people of the sickened country he so hated, Adam's ready response took me aback. He said he could never live in such miserable fashion, the very thought of Afghanistan was torture. That wasn't his type of jihad. It was the inner struggle that mattered. The everyday wrestling matches with your fallibility as a human being.

Bravo Adam. In this sense, there was no doubt in my mind that we were comrades.

After unpacking, Adam and I lounge a la comrade style in wicker chairs scattered around the hotel's shady garden. We order some tea. Then I notice a bushy haired man adjusting a tripod on the driveway and peering into a huge telephoto lens. He waves in our direction. Adam chooses to ignore him and when I ask why, I'm duly informed that the guy is some sort of scam artist working for the World Wildlife Organization office in Gilgit.

"You don't want to have anything to do with him," Adam advises. "He'll wow you with all kinds of promises, but he's just one of those flashy NGO types who knows how to sweet talk foreigners and have them eating out of his palm."

I stiffly rise and make my way to the scam artist.

"Don't say I didn't warn you!" Adam shouts.

"Hi there!"

Mr. NGO/Scam Artist offers a gummy smile.

"You're from the USA, am I right? Wait. Wait. Let me guess. Illinois, Indiana, Michigan?"

I shake my head.

"Wait. Wait. Don't tell me! Colorado, right? You look like a Colorado girl."

Mr. NGO/Scam Artist gestures at my REI water bottle with the stainless steel carabineer clip ring and mumbles to himself.

"They all have one of those things."

"I'm from Washington State," I reply. "Seattle's my hometown."

"But I thought Seattle is in Canada!"

"No not quite. We're close to the border, but we're very much American."

"Seattle, Seattle. Ah yes, Seattle!"

"Have you been there?"

"Golly! I'd love to!"

"It rains a lot."

"You are birthplace of Microsoft. Am I right?"

"I guess so."

"You are knowing Mr. Bill Gates. Am I right?"

"Sort of."

"Wonderful! How very wonderful!"

Mr. NGO/Scam Artist licks his lips and presents me with a business card. It displays the World Wildlife logo of a panda bear and his job title as Project Manager.

"May I have a look at your camera?"

"By all means."

I stand on my tiptoes and look into the Nikon lens. A close up appears of Adam sipping his chai and staring in my direction ever so smugly. I swing the tripod toward the mountains in the backdrop. They are heaven like and mysterious. The trek seems promising. I plan to turn into bed early tonight and get plenty of rest.

"Thank you so much."

We shake hands and before the WWO activist or NGO nitwit or scammer or whoever he is has a chance to ask me any further questions, I steadily walk back towards Adam who is by now chatting with a trio of policemen. The chairs have been rearranged in a circle under the canopy of an almond tree. The cops keep their rifles lengthwise in their laps. Everyone smiles as I approach and salute them smartly.

"We have been talking about you," Adam says and winks.

He's wearing his favorite hat, the one with the pancake flat top and shallow brim. He only wears it when he's in a good mood, so I take his comment in stride.

"They have been asking questions," Adam continues. "They want to know what you're doing here all by yourself. I told them what I think. You are some sort of American agent. CIA. FBI. No. Not FBI. You can't even walk on a suspension bridge. I bet the CIA hired you because of all your languages. They sent you in the field because you look Pakistani. You think you've gone undercover but you don't fool me. Not even for a minute. Nobody messes with Adam Khan. Nobody!"

Dear me. He's really overdoing it probably just to impress the cops. They keep smiling at me and I particularly like the twinkle of the green eyed cop who introduces himself as Hossein.

"He's Shia," Adam says as though it wasn't obvious. I'm not sure if I want to get into religion with Adam. The last time it came up, he went on and on about the Karbala martyrdom of Hasan and Hossein. They were grandsons of the Prophet Muhammad from his daughter Fatima's marriage to Ali who is so revered by the Shias that instead of saying *Ya Allah*, as in God give me strength, they say *Ya Ali, Ya Ali*.

I grew up hearing all this as a child in Karachi. My grandmother, though Suni like me and the rest of our family, was somehow partial to Shia rituals and I would attend with her religious ceremonies to mourn and lament the events of Karbala during the month of Muharram. These ceremonies were raw with emotion, with passions overflowing and it's the same passion that I see in Adam's retelling of the Karbala massacre as though he had personally witnessed the gruesome murders that took place there in the seventh century.

One time, Adam spoke with so much fervor about what it meant to be Shia that he convinced me to convert. I had sympathy and compassion for the martyred, I couldn't deny the wisdom and ideals of Hazrat Ali, plus I was familiar with the Shia rituals, so it was just silly of me not to make it official.

Adam knew a famous sheikh in Gilgit. He would see to it that I was properly indoctrinated. It would be our top priority once we got back. We had to return to Gilgit anyhow. It had a sizeable Shia community. I would be in good hands.

My mind was almost made up that this conversion would be pretty harmless. I would still be a Muslim. I didn't think my family would mind as long as I kept praying and observing Ramadan. Though I'm not sure what they would have thought had they seen me hobnobbing in the secluded backwoods of Northern Pakistan with this dubious male quartet, three of them police officers with loaded guns on their thighs, the other, a smart aleck know it all prince who suspects me of being a spook and is planning to get me converted into his sect just because I like his storytelling style.

"Can you take a picture of us?"

I hand Adam my beat up Rollei. Even if I don't live to tell this tale to my parents or my future offspring, at least they will have proof that it wasn't just an elaborate fabrication. The policemen don't mind the indulgence. They take off their caps and pose for the camera, their legs crossed on one knee. I copy the move. Then we all stand with me in the middle of the group. Adam clicks away. I tell him to zoom in for a close up. Seeing will lead to believing.

We ask the cops to stay for dinner, but after patrolling the area all day, they're eager to be off duty and return to Gilgit to their wives and children. Tomorrow will be a new beat in a new location. Nothing exciting going on, but you never know in these parts.

The lack of any company makes for a tedious meal. It's just Adam, me and the driver in the hotel's empty dining hall and I'm picking at my *daal* which smells a bit rancid and they have run out of bread so there's not much else to eat.

"Here take this."

Adam shoves his plate of rice in my direction. I ask for some yogurt and blend it together in a gooey paste which tastes more edible.

"We'll get more provisions in the morning," the driver informs.

"Don't worry. You won't starve," Adam chirps in. "You'll have the time of your life."

8

SPY GIRL

Upper Hunza, July 2003

THE TAGAPHARI TRAIL BEGINS from just behind the hotel as we ascend a steep ridge in the bright glare of the midday sun. The plan had been to wake up by five in the morning and get the bulk of our climbing done in the cooler morning hours. But my alarm clock had remained mute and I overslept as did Adam and the driver. In spite of the burning heat and the late start, no one is complaining and the hike so far is enjoyable, testing my limits ever so slightly with its tight switchbacks and narrow drop-offs, but nothing that I haven't seen before and cannot handle. The total altitude we will gain until Rakaposhi base camp is about four thousand feet which will be made easier by splitting the hike into two days with four to five hours of walking each day. Our goal for today is to walk about six kilometers until the midway point at Hapakun.

Adam assures me that we will easily get there by sundown. He's being super casual about the whole expedition, even though this is our most challenging hike in terms of distance and a first when it comes to camping in the backcountry. We have borrowed sleeping bags and tents from the hotel and a lightweight propane stove. The weather is supposed to be mild. Even more miraculous, Adam and I are in sync having put away our boxing gloves, at least for today. After trekking for an hour and a half, we take a break at a makeshift tea house by a cool mountain stream.

A small boned boy, about eight or nine years old, fills up water in a rusty kettle and sets it to boil on a fire composed of twigs. His mother offers us some bread, a denser, chewier type of *naan* that seems to expand in the stomach. We are soon joined by a Japanese couple, one of the few foreigners I have seen in Pakistan. They say hello and offer us rice cakes as we share with them the ghee drenched *aloo parathas* the hotel staff has supplied us for lunch.

A bunch of local kids approach our party and I snap pictures of Adam fooling around with them. In one frame, he is wearing one of those funny glasses attached to a rubber nose and mustache. In another shot, Adam is squatting and holding two squirmy boys on either side as one of them holds up his fingers in the victory sign behind Adam's head. The kids soon get bored and gravitate towards the Japanese pair. They are busy tinkering around with some fancy camera equipment. There are some rickety wooden huts in the distance that look abandoned. When I go to inspect them up close, Adam points out the writing someone has chalked on one of the tattered doors. It reads Coca Cola in Urdu. All of a sudden, Adam slides up close and whispers in my ears.

"Jasous!"

"Will you stop already? How many times do I have to tell you that I'm not a spy!"

Adam laughs as though he doesn't believe a word. He tells me to hurry along. We still have five more kilometers to go and half the day is gone already.

"It's not my fault the alarm clock didn't work," I whine. "It was cheap quality, a total piece of junk from the Gilgit bazaar."

"It would have worked just fine if you knew how to use it," Adam chides. "You probably forgot to press the button to set the alarm buzzer."

"Button, what button?"

"My point exactly."

I had to let him win this one. I was a complete idiot when it came to gadgets.

We resume our trek along the Minapin River and then through a juniper forest. To ease my burden, the driver is carrying my pack along with his own rucksack containing our camping gear. Adam and I are walking side by side, but I'm getting tired listening to him going on and on about the spying business and how he's going to blow my cover. I start slowing down. Adam marches ahead. We regroup at Bang-i-Das where there's a small waterfall at the head of a pleasant green valley. The sun is merciless and I rest under a shady grove on a terraced slope. Adam and the driver are taking a cigarette break on the slope just below. I tell them that I need the bathroom and go off in search of a discreet shelter.

When I get back to my spot, Adam and the driver are no longer there. As I walk around the slope searching for them, my head starts spinning and I feel limp from a sudden drop in my blood sugar level. I'm longing for a candy bar, even just a sip of water, but my bottle is with the driver. And so is all my food. I'm feeling more and more light headed. There is no sign of Adam and the driver. I begin to panic and call for them at the top of my lungs. There is no response. Where could they be? Surely they couldn't have just vanished. Or did they? Maybe the myths are real and some evil jinn turned them into fairy dust. Or maybe this is Adam's idea of a practical joke. Just wait till I get my hands on Mr. Mountain Expert. I'm going to wring his princely neck out for abandoning me like this. I feel around in my pockets for an energy bar, apricots, walnuts, anything that I can munch on to get reenergized. But there's nothing except for some crumpled tissues.

"ADAM!! AD-DAM!!!"

"WHERE ARE YOU??!!"

He really has become fairy dust. So has the driver.

I decide to wait fifteen more minutes by which time they would surely emerge. It is impossible to find any shade so I just recline on the grass and roast. I roll down the sleeves of my *kurta* and unfurl my scarf so that it covers my head and face. Through the thin cotton fabric, I turn my face directly into the sun and try to stare straight at it without blinking just as I used to as a child. I'm over powered by white hot light. It's like staring into an abyss. There is no beginning, no end. There is only this light, this sky, this air, these trees, these mountains and and…I snatch the scarf off my face and look around wildly. There is no one around. There is no sound. Not even any birds. But the silence is deafening. It blares into my ears and I can't escape it.

My watch reads 3:30 PM. I have lost all sense of time. It feels like days since I set off on this trek. There is still no trace of Adam and the driver. Instead of waiting any longer, I decide to head down the mountain alone. If I stay any longer, I am bound to faint from hunger and who knows when I'll be found in this deserted valley. I'm not sure that I know the way back, but I need to move and abort the panic button. I begin scrambling down the path we came up and follow the stream until the tea house. The mother and small boy are still there. They have not seen the missing duo.

I plead with the boy to take me back to the hotel for a substantial fee--three hundred Rupees. I can give him more if he wants. I'm ready to give him whatever price he wants. The boy looks at his mother. She gives a slight nod and soon we are off. I follow my little Shepherd's steady gait with my eyes peeled at a tree bark staff in his right hand. His presence is reassuring. Even if I do faint from hunger, at least there will be a witness. Come on, come on, I tell myself. Don't cave now. You can do this. I swallow great big gulps of air. The boy turns around and checks on me. I give him the thumbs up sign. It's OK. I'm going to be OK.

An hour later, we are winding our way down the switchbacks. I breathe a sigh of relief at the familiar landscape. The gold and green patchwork of fields, the raging river and pinkish granite walls of the mountainside. My chaperone leads me straight towards the hotel's front door which he refuses to enter. I slip the money in his half torn shirt pocket and he runs off.

Nobody is at the front desk. Then one of the errand boys saunters into the lobby in his flip flops and looks at me blankly. He's joined by another errand boy and neither of them are the slightest bit concerned that I have separated from my hiking party who are still missing. Not even the manager seems to care. I hate them all. I hate their lackadaisical manners and their molasses walk and their blank poker faces. They are all just standing around staring at me. I am longing for a glass of water and a hunk of bread. The manager hands me a menu. Just bring me everything you have in the fridge, I tell one of the boys. He brings me some leftovers from lunch and a pitcher of orange juice. My head stops spinning and I retire to my room to shower and pray and wait. Three hours later there's a knock at my door. It's the driver. His hiking clothes are streaked with dirt. His vacant eyes look slightly haunted. I'm seeing an orange haired ghost.

"Where have you been?" he asks in Urdu. "We've been looking everywhere for you."

I can't get the words out fast enough.

"Where have I been?? Where have I been?? I have been waiting for you two, only you and his Majesty did not bother to show up, that's all. I almost died up there!"

"What are you talking about? Adam and I have been searching for you for the last two hours. That boy has been worried sick about you. We thought you fell off the mountain and broke your leg. How could you just disappear like that without telling us?"

"But I told you I was going to the bathroom! When I came down, you had both gone."

"We didn't go anywhere."

"But you did, I tell you! I looked everywhere and I couldn't find you and Adam. Didn't you hear me? I kept calling for you."

"No."

"That's strange."

"This is a rotten way to treat us. We've taken such good care of you. Adam is furious. He won't let you get away with this."

"Get away with what? I haven't done anything!"

The driver shrugs his shoulders and I ask him to leave. It's no use talking to him. I only want to speak with Adam. Alone. He doesn't even bother to knock. He barges right into my room and flings himself in a chair leaving the door wide open. His eyes are a cauldron of fire. We have a shouting match in front of the entire hotel staff. There are no other guests, but even if there were, I couldn't have cared if we were seen or heard. Adam is being impossible. He's convinced that I had abandoned the group on purpose and now I'm lying about it and trying to deceive them. According to Adam Khan, I'm up to no good and he's going to report me to the local authorities.

It has all gone horribly wrong. I've never seen Adam so angry. I can't trust him anymore. Regardless of what he does, I wouldn't be able to prove my identity. Both my passports are in Karachi, locked in Suraya Aunty's safe deposit box. I can't show any evidence of being American or Pakistani. If they really take me for a spy, I'm going to have no immunity whatsoever without documentation. It's not a good situation.

"I'm tired," I say. "I really need some sleep."

"Go on. Get all the sleep you need. You won't be getting much rest after tonight."

Adam's voice is laced with sarcasm. There he goes again scaring me silly with his big talk.

"Good night then."

I close my door and lock it just before crawling into bed. My head is spinning again, but this time it is not just hunger pangs. I am terrified of being trapped in this Shangri-La which has morphed from paradise into my own personal hell.

* * *

There is a mosquito in my room and he won't leave me alone. I pull the covers over my face and burrow in the shade, but I can still hear the sucker. He's going to drive me mad unless I blot out his tiny existence so I grab my shoe and try in vain to slam it against the wall. BANG! It's no use. Now the sucker is behind my head and I turn around and aim for him again. BANG!! Oh I almost had him. How I wish that Adam was the mosquito. I still cannot fathom why that boy has such a hold on me. I'm sick of his pompous airs and all his accusations. BANG!! Victory at last. There's a smear of blood on the wall which I don't bother to clean up.

I get back in bed and will myself to fall asleep. My eyes are wide open. There's too much to think about and worry. The day's paranoia is gradually dissipating, but not without a sense of dread. I am still in the grip of one of my biggest fears. Entrapment. I keep reminding myself that this is not my real life. This is not even my country any longer. Haven't I seen it all?

The following morning I wake up at nine having slept fitfully for about three hours. Adam and the driver are eating scrambled eggs and toast in the dining hall. They smile at me as I take a seat. There's an atmosphere of sunny blue skies after a raging tempest. We have nothing to say to each other, nothing more to explain.

Escape. I yearn for escape. When I bring up the subject, Adam has a resolute plan. They will drop me off in Gilgit where I'll board the afternoon bus bound for Rawalpindi. It will take about fifteen hours, more if the roads are bad.

Fifteen hours. Fifteen days. It makes no difference to me. As long as I can flee this sequestered paradise. Two weeks ago, I was begging to be here. Now I can't wait to get away.

What about my conversion Adam wants to know. Didn't I want to become a Shia and go through the rites in Gilgit. I tell him that I'm not going through with any of it. I've had my share of excitement on this trip. Enough to sustain me for a long, long time. Adam laughs rather too hard. I know what he's thinking. Spy girl is chickening out. She's far too much of a coward.

I stifle a smile. That's a matter of pure contention, Adam Khan. But let's not hash it out now. Let it be reserved for another lifetime.

9

MUGHAL MADNESS

Lahore, August, 2003

I SEE HER AS SOON AS I WALK into the baggage claim area of Lahore's Allama Iqbal International She has a stocky frame, a bit on the plumpish side and her light brown hair is getting thinner. It's the tight lipped smile that I remember the most and the sharp, inquisitive hazel eyes. She is short like me so I don't need to stand on my tip toes when we hug. I get enveloped in her soft breasts and inhale a whiff of lavender eau de cologne in the folds of her soft cotton *dupatta*. She waves to a porter to pick up my luggage and then ushers us into the parking lot where there is a waiting car and driver. It's all very fast and efficient and so very un-Pakistani. But Tahira Aunty wouldn't have it any other way.

It was *Bari Phupi,* my aunt in Seattle who had put me in touch with her. The two of them had been best friends and gone to school together at St. Joseph's, a Karachi convent for girls. Knowing that I would end up in Lahore at some point in my journey, I had requested Tahira Aunty's phone number and email address and written to her when I was in Karachi. It was a rather pompous, long winded email elaborating on my field research plans with the Human Rights Commission of Pakistan based in Lahore. I was going to investigate the Hudood Ordinances, a series of controversial laws in dealing with rape crimes. I went on and on about the oppressiveness of the Pakistani legal system, the denial of civil liberties and the inherent gender biases. It was far too long for an email, but it was intentional.

My goal was to impress Tahira Aunty with my academic credentials, something she would value as a teacher at the Lahore American High School. The last thing I wanted was for her to take me for a wander lusting vagabond flirting with danger and death by frolicking around in the hinterlands of Pakistan. So there was no mention of my solo adventures in Peshawar or the Khyber Pass jeep drive and the gunsmith's bazaar, not even a hint of that eventful weekend in Mansehra where I had run off with the servants and danced at a village wedding. It was tempting to tell her about my tryst with royalty and the Karakoram road trip, but it wasn't going to be easy explaining Adam Khan and our mountain madness, so that too remained undisclosed.

I must have created a favorable impression for Tahira Aunty offered to take me in as a house guest which I gladly accepted.

"You look remarkably the same. Of course I haven't seen you since you were ten years old but you haven't changed all that much. It's all in the eyes. Yours are just the same. To a tee! But you've grown far too thin. We're going to have to fatten you up. Otherwise, your Seattle aunt will think we are starving you in Lahore. Oh Khalid! Do stop at the bakery on the way home. And turn up the AC. I'm sure our guest from Boston finds it much too hot for her liking."

"I'm OK. It's not that bad. I've gotten used to the heat."

"My dear girl! You're being far too polite. I know you Americans like your comfort. You carry pillows on the plane and you have your Birkenstocks. Excellent shoes by the way."

"I think Birkenstocks are German. I've never worn them. And I don't have a pillow for the plane. I just use my jacket."

"What was that my dear?"

"Nothing.

"You'll have to speak up more. My hearing is not as good these days. Of course, your Uncle thinks I should get it checked. If it were up to Rafiq, I'd be at the bloody doctor's office every day of the week. One day it's my ears. The next it will be my eyesight. Then my blood pressure. It has been on the high side lately. But I'm taking precaution by starting a low salt diet. Why just the other day I told

Nawaz to cook my rice separately, just plain water and a bit of *haldi*
for color. I think I'm going to teach the boy how to make risotto next.
Ah here we are. Khalid, get us three loaves of white bread and some
lemon pound cake. What's that my dear? Very well. One extra loaf of
whole meal bread, Khalid, for our guest. And do hurry along. I must
be back at the school after lunch time."

While we are waiting in the back seat of the car, Tahira Aunty
reaches into her purse and hands me a book.

"You were quite a bookworm in Karachi. I brought you
something you might like. He is one of our best."

It's a thin volume of short stories by Sadat Hasan Manto
translated into English.

"Thank you. Thank you so much. You needn't have gone to so
much trouble."

"Not at all my dear."

Her gesture is touching and promptly erases all my irritation
with Tahira Aunty as a crabby chatter box who has me figured out
all wrong. But I'm still going to have to set her straight on the
comfort seeking American bit.

The driver returns with the bread and we are off again heading
to Tahira Aunty's house. From what she had told me in her email,
Tahira Aunty and her husband live in the Railway Officers Colony
near Lahore's Walton Railway Station. The traffic gets more congested
and the noise factor increases with all the motor rickshaws chugging
along the road. Every city has its soundtrack and I'm already
composing Lahore's with this putt putting throb that seeps into my ears,
making me impervious to anything else that might warrant attention.

Their house is a large cement bungalow on the corner of a dirt lane.
It has a lush front garden with marigolds and hibiscus flowers in bloom.
A pudgy Saint Bernard comes out to the driveway and slobbers all
over Tahira Aunty. I keep my distance as I'm not a dog lover ever
since I was bitten by a German Shepherd as a child. Tahira Aunty
picks up on my tension and keeps the creature at a safe distance.

"Where is everyone?" she hollers in Urdu.

"Nawaz! Ghazala!"

A crew of servants dash to the front door. They look at me with
hesitation as if not quite sure what to make of this diminutive creature

stooped under the weight of a tanker sized pack strapped to her back. One of them offers to carry my bag. He looks me straight in the eye and smiles. I smile back and for a moment we stare at each other in the curious manner of children appraising a newcomer in the classroom.

"Nawaz, take these things in the kitchen. And bring us some chai and buttered toast. Come along my dear. Let me show you to your room."

I follow Tahira Aunty inside the house and we climb a shallow staircase that leads to a large rectangular hallway that is empty except for an ironing board and a laundry basket stacked with clothes. Tahira Aunty opens one of the doors adjoining the hallway and ushers me into a spacious bedroom furnished with a full sized bed, a large desk next to the air conditioner and built in wall closets.

"The *loo* is this way."

Tahira Aunty steps into a smaller connecting room with a bureau and full length mirror. She opens another door and points out a large, sparkling tiled bathroom. I'm thrilled with the prospect of having all this luxury entirely to myself. No more rowdy roommates. No charpoys in country villages. No vacant hotels and lodges in remote mountain wilderness. A girl can get downright spoiled living this way.

* * *

The following morning I am awakened by a loud knock. Nawaz is standing just outside my bedroom with a steaming mug of chai. *Chota hazri,* the English used to call it. I take the tea from Nawaz and thank him.

"Breakfast ready," he says. "Uncle waiting for you."

Nawaz shifts his weight from one foot to the other mindful of the invisible fence between us. He is young and handsome with a cute pug nose, gleaming, brown eyes and skin the color of fine, dark chocolate. His English is not very good and even in his Urdu, there's a hint of an accent. I ask Nawaz where he's from.

"Thatta," he replies with a shy grin.

A Sindhi boy. Close to Karachi. I like that. He has an honest, trusting face and every time he smiles at me, his eyes sparkle and shine as though they're trying to tell me that we might just be long lost friends.

"I'll be downstairs in ten minutes," I declare and gently close the door.

The breakfast table is set for two. There's a pot of tea and a rack of burnt toast next to a porcelain dish of marmalade. A silver haired man eyes me from the top of a newspaper. He is older than I had expected, somewhere in his mid to late sixties. Tahira Aunty was obviously much younger, but that didn't seem to deter her from taking the upper hand and criticizing her husband's remarks the way she had done on our taxi ride from the airport. She's not around, but her lavender scent perfumes the dining room which is dark and quiet with all the curtains drawn to keep the house cool.

"Have a seat my dear," Rafiq Uncle says. "Tahira had to attend a meeting at school. She'll be back by one for lunch. Do help yourself. We have eggs. Nawaz! Bring the memsahib some eggs, there's a good fellow. How would you like them, my dear?"

"Scrambled, please."

"Scrambled," he yells into the kitchen.

I pour myself a cup of tea. It is already mixed with milk and sugar and far too lukewarm for my taste. But I gulp it down just to have something to do.

"So, my dear. How are you enjoying your visit to Pakistan? Tahira tells me you have come back after quite some time. Eleven years is it?

"Twenty one."

"My my. That is quite a stretch."

I munch on the burnt toast.

"What a lot of changes you must have witnessed. Of course, nothing ever changes in Pakistan. Old wine in new bottles. That's how we operate for the most part."

Rafiq Uncle laughs and we look at each other and smile politely. I like his simple clothes, a snow white cotton *kurta* and matching pajama. He has an interesting face, strong boned and manly with a slender straight nose and light gray eyes that are full of mirth and mischief.

A sullen faced girl with sharp cut features highlighted with too much makeup brings my plate of eggs and hurries back into the kitchen. Her demeanor suggests that ferrying food to the table is a labor far too menial for someone with her looks and the ambition that goes along with them. For a moment, I'm reminded of my roommate Momina whose effortless beauty had initially placed her in the haughty club of Pakistani prima donnas until I was won over by her charm and sassiness. But this girl has none of Momina's talents.

"That's Ghazala," says Rafiq Uncle. "One of the servant's daughters. We took them in when she was just a baby. She's a bit of a brat now. But don't let that get to you."

Easier said than done I think watching Ghazala fidgeting by my side and chewing her nails.

"So what's your agenda for the rest of the day?"

Rafiq Uncle puts away his newspaper and looks at me straight in the eyes. Though I scarcely know him, there is something about his gaze that makes me want to confide in him. I like his forthright manner that is so different from his wife's because it feels less judgmental. I know that I'm still under inspection having just arrived in their house as a single young girl with no apparent purpose, but Rafiq Uncle is not the probing type which is precisely why I like him so much.

"I need to attend to some work."

"Work, what work? Don't tell me you've come all this way to sequester yourself in some dingy old office!"

I explain to Rafiq Uncle that my errand concerns the Human Rights Commission of Pakistan. They have offered me a formal internship, but the idea of getting tied up with a nine to five desk job in Lahore doesn't seem so appealing. I only have a month and a half left before my return to Boston and graduate school. I'm hoping to remain footloose and somehow manage to do my research at the same time. Rafiq Uncle informs me the office is far away when I show him the address I need to get to.

"You'll have to take a taxi," he says.

I interpret this to mean that they're too cheap to lend me their car and waste its precious petrol on my behalf. It's my errand so it's my responsibility to fulfill it. I'm all for independence. But I still think it's petty minded to be counting rupees on gas expense when they can afford imported luxuries like a Whirlpool washing machine and dryer that I had spotted upstairs in the hallway outside my room.

"I think I'll go up to my room and have a lie down," I announce rising from my chair.

"Excellent idea my dear. Get all the rest you need," Rafiq Uncle replies and buries his face behind the newspaper crisply folded in half. "See you at lunchtime," he adds.

I take the stairs two at a time and collapse on the bed like a fallen angel, my energy already depleting. My thoughts drift back to Rafiq Uncle. I don't know much about his background other than what Tahira Aunty had told me on the car ride from the airport. Her husband is a retired engineer from the Pakistani railways. His family hails from India from the northern state of Uttar Pradesh. They had come to Lahore during the bloodbath of partition which was made even more volatile when the Punjab was split between two countries. Lahore, which was once the heartland of the Indian Mughal Empire, ended up in Pakistan and places like Amritsar with a predominant Sikh community became a part of India. The consequences were disastrous.

Muslims, Hindus, Christians, Sikhs, who had been neighbors and friends for years living together in peace and harmony respecting each other's differences, became enemies overnight. Massive riots turned the streets into an inferno as people killed each other in the name of religion. Trainloads of refugees would arrive at stations with bloody corpses. The sudden and arbitrary nature of the newly drawn borders gave way to the biggest migration in human history with over fourteen million souls transferring from India to Pakistan and vice versa.

There's so much I want to ask Rafiq Uncle about this painful topic, but I don't know where to start or how to broach it without bruising our emotional scars. Even though I did not make the physical crossing that he undertook, that my parents did when they left their native landmarks of Bombay and Bangalore for Karachi, I am nonetheless a product of partition, a child of divided loyalties whose very existence was born out of breakage.

In 1971, the year of my birth, Pakistan was in the throes of a bitter civil war. My parents told me stories of how they used to stuff my ear with cotton balls and we would all crouch under the dining table while Pakistani and Indian jets roared above our house in dogfights. It became routine to hear air raid sirens and cover windows with blackout paper. The worst thing about the war was the closure of the Indian/Pakistani border. It was hard on my mother since she had to leave behind all her family in Bombay upon marrying my father who was already a Karachi resident. My mother had to change nationalities and revoke her Indian citizenship for a Pakistani passport. Living on the other side of the border in the aftermath of war meant that she couldn't take her first born to see her grandparents, aunts, uncles and cousins because they resided in enemy territory.

I was five years old when I first met my Indian relatives at Bombay's Santa Cruz airport. I still remember my mother's four sisters who I referred to as my *khalas* pinching my cheeks with affection. They all wore the *churidar* and *kurta*, skin tight trousers scrunched at the ankles paired with form fitting knee length tunics with long side slits. Nanijan, my maternal grandmother, wore her trademark sari, her yellow-gray hair coiled up in a low bun. She approached my father who lowered his head to accept the garland of flowers that perfumed his suit with the scent of jasmine and roses. There was another garland for my mother followed by a tearful hug.

A bare foot porter wheeled our luggage into the blazing Indian heat. Then we were off to my grandmother's apartment near Bombay Central train station. And it was this Bombay apartment where I ended up spending most of my summer holidays while growing up in Karachi. The thing I loved best about Nanijan's place was the open roof top terrace where every morning I fed the pigeons my *puran poli* scraps. In addition to the sugary pancakes made with chickpea flour, my taste buds developed a passion for *bhindi ki sabzi, karela, jinghay palao, bombal machi, chanwal ki roti*. Okra, bitter gourd, shrimp paella, dry salted fish and flatbread with crushed rice. They were pungent, spicy dishes cooked in the Kokni style of coastal India in the state of Maharashtra. My mother had retained some of the Kokni language from her childhood. It was similar to the Marathi that she spoke with Parvati, the servant woman who came to my grandmother's house every day to sweep and chop vegetables for the day's cooking.

Parvati wore a small red dot in the middle of her forehead and her frayed cotton sari was bunched up to her knees with the ends

gathered between her legs. Her skin was the shade of darkly roasted
espresso beans minus the smooth texture and she liked to hold up
her forearm against mine and compare our different colors. It was
not just Parvati, but my cousins who were obsessed with my
fairness. I was nicknamed *gori mem*, white lady. I was expected to
bathe with milk. It pained me to be treated as different. I wanted to
show my Indian cousins that I was just like them and being Pakistani
did not exactly make me an alien however much it was desired by
the powers that be.

As children, our identities were still loose and malleable and
soon we would be eating mangoes together and playing silly dress
up games with the contents of Nanijan's *almari*, a huge teak closet
that took up an entire bedroom wall. I would hook a silver *tikka* on
the side of my hair and slip into a billowy *gharara* skirt. It was
supposed to make me look like a Begum from Lucknow. My cousin
Mona took a tie dye *dupatta* and tied it like a sari. She painted a dot
on the middle of her forehead with a mascara wand and called
herself a fisherman's wife. Her elder brother nicknamed Guddoo
wore a too big safari suit and a wicker basket for a hat. I curtsied and
called him *saab*. Mona gave him a mustache with an eyebrow pencil.

From shopping sprees in Colaba to catching the latest Bollywood
film at Maratha Mandir Theater, there was never a lack of things to
do in Bombay. My favorite outing was going to the Hanging Gardens
just above Malabar Hill with Zeba Khala, the most sophisticated and
cultured of my aunts. We would wander through the park naming
all the animals that were carved out of hedges. If I was on my best
behavior, there would be a special treat of *bhel puris* at Chowpatty
Beach. Then we would head home by riding one of the cherry red
double decker buses from Flora Fountain to Breech Candy where
my aunt liked to buy tea rose perfume from a department store
known as Benzer's.

Bombay was as familiar to me as Karachi. Those back and forth
trips across the Arabian Sea, a distance of roughly five hundred
miles, cemented the feeling of belonging to both places and as I grew
up in America, I found it increasingly hard to talk about Pakistan
without mentioning India. It was complicated to explain all the
connections and I started envying all the first and second generation

South Asians I eventually met in college. They did not share my geographical fault lines. It all started with partition. It should never have happened. I have a broken identity. I come from a broken land.

* * *

The following day, Tahira Aunty decides to take the morning off to accompany me to the Human Rights Commission of Pakistan. When I tell her that I was planning on going to their office by taxi as proposed by her husband yesterday, Tahira Aunty shoos away the idea as ludicrous. I must take the family car and driver. It is the proper thing to do. And she will be delighted to come along. I suspect she is only being so generous on account of being a fan of HRCP director I.A. Rehman with whom I have a meeting. I don't know much about Rehman, but the mere mention of his name turns Tahira Aunty into a star struck groupie, which makes me think he must be a bit of a celebrity among Pakistani intellectuals and progressive minded liberals.

"So how is Pakistan treating you so far?"

"Not too badly, thank you."

"Welcome. Welcome. Have a seat."

"*Assalam Alaikum.*"

"Sit sit. No need to be so formal."

I.A. Rehman sits across from us behind a large wooden desk. The first thing I notice is the look in his eyes that tells me this is a man who has seen it all. I like his character filled face and easy going manners. Unlike most intellectuals I've come across, Pakistani or otherwise, Rehman uses words sparingly with the utmost economy as though he has only a handful at his disposal and must ration them with care.

We briefly discuss the premise of my graduate thesis which is on the Islamization of laws in Pakistan during the Zia era focusing primarily on the Hudood Ordinance, a heinous law that is still on Pakistani statute books after it was introduced in 1979. Under this law, a woman who has been raped is automatically accused of adultery if she cannot prove the rape by having four Muslim males witness the actual act. Since this is virtually impossible, rape victims in Pakistan are charged with the crime of extra-marital sex punishable either by lashes, jail or stoning to death. One of the biggest problems with Hudood is in regards to interpretation. In my thesis, I will attempt to prove the very un-Islamic nature of this allegedly Islamic law that was in large part wielded for political reasons.

Tahira Aunty keeps nodding her head as if to punctuate each of my words with an exclamation point. Rehman pays no attention to her. He looks at me instead.

"Plenty of literature on the topic. You can start your work here as soon as you wish."

Now that I have such a gracious offer, it seems silly to tell him that I don't want to be chained to a desk for eight hours a day to do research, that I'd rather be a free agent milling about Lahore and using their facilities and library on my own schedule. It's an unpaid internship and Rehman seems rather lax about it not talking about hours or what is expected of me in terms of output. I want to keep it this way to avoid any excessive commitments. Of course, I realize how flaky this all sounds.

"Thank you so much. It is most kind of you."

"The pleasure is all mine."

I.A. Rehman extends his right palm and we shake hands. It's a firm solid grasp. Tahira Aunty gushes forward to duplicate the gesture.

"It's been most delightful!"

Next thing, she'll be asking for an autograph.

"Not at all. Not at all."

Rehman presses a buzzer on his desk and a man opens the door to escort us out. I decide to stay at the office while Tahira Aunty returns to the waiting car with a look of disappointment, as though she had gotten the backstage pass only to have failed to make a lasting impression. I feel a bit sorry for her. She really did admire the man and wanted to be taken seriously. But then again, maybe she just wanted to be in the limelight because that's what she's used to. I tell Tahira Aunty that I'll make my own way back to the house. Taxi or rickshaw, I'll figure it out. Tahira Aunty writes down her address in Urdu just in case my English is incomprehensible to Lahore's cabbies or rickshaw-wallahs. For some reason, she keeps forgetting that I can read, write and speak Urdu. It's our first language. Yet, we converse exclusively in English which denotes on us the rank of civilized people.

"I need a what?" I ask dumfounded.

"*Chit. Chit. Tumharee chit kidar hay? Chit kay baghair paper na mil sak ta.*"

The peon at the archive department is saying that I need a small piece of paper to authorize my access to read a local newspaper article. I tell him that I just need to read the one article about a protest rally to overturn the Hudood Ordinance by the Woman's Action Forum, one of Pakistan's most active lobbying groups on behalf of women. I can read it in front of him if he's afraid I'll pinch the paper. He tells me I'm not getting my hands on any paper without the aforementioned chit. I ask him from whom do I get this chit. The Managing Director, I'm duly informed. But she is not in the office today. I will have to come back tomorrow. With the chit the man stresses, folding his arms with a veneer of authority that clearly relishes my frustration. I feel utterly useless as I return to the small office they have given me which is shared by two other girls.

Sania is a pretty Lahori and the office IT expert. Catherine, a tall blond Canadian has been working at HRCP as a summer intern. I'm impressed to learn that she's a house guest of Asma Jehangir, the renowned Pakistani human rights lawyer who is apparently a prisoner in her own home these days. There are rumors of death threats. The mullahs and jihadis are having a field day. Catherine looks grim and fearful. I tell her that she is blowing it all out of proportion. Exactly what part are you having trouble understanding, the death threats or the jihadi elements that are taking this country back to the Stone Age is Catherine's take. We argue back and forth. Sania remains a silent spectator. I make a mental note of her stylish outfit. A tight fitting knee length kurta with extra long side slits paired with slim trousers grazing the ankle. The argument peters out. Catherine turns her back to me and taps away on her laptop. I take that as my cue and leave the premises.

* * *

My mind is full of air. For the past few weeks, I've been cocooned in my room all morning while attempting to read and write with the air conditioner droning full blast. Attempt is the key word. In the last four hours, I have typed just half a page. It shouldn't be this difficult now that I have some good research material thanks to a small library that I was able to access sans chit. My thesis will flesh out quite nicely with all this local data. There is so much to say, but I don't know how to say it. I cannot write. I cannot think. I cannot do a thing in Lahore except vegetate in this house that is starting to feel more and more like a fortress.

Tahira Aunty will not let me explore the town on my own and I'm too tired and drained to pick up a guidebook and figure it all out. I want to be babysat in these few remaining weeks. If only there was someone by my side to show me the sights, navigate all the logistics of getting from A to B, so that all I have to do is to come along for the ride and savor the journey's parting moments. If only.

There is one bright spot to being in Lahore and that is my cooking sessions with Nawaz. He has taken to knocking at my door precisely at one in the afternoon so I can take a break from my pathetic work and accompany him to the kitchen downstairs where I'm learning how to make *rotis,* homemade tortillas from scratch. I've been buying *rotis* in cellophane packets at ethnic grocery stores all these years in the States. But now I get to experience the real thing. Nawaz brings home fresh flour in a paper bag still warm from being ground in the mill. Then he mixes it with some water for the dough and shows me how to scoop it out with my fingers and make a *pera* that resembles a disc the size of a hockey puck that we will flatten out with a rolling pin. My *pera* turns out horribly uneven compared to Nawaz's smooth rounded edges. He tells me I'm getting better at it, but I know it's a lie when Rafiq Uncle picks out a *roti* from a cloth covered pile that looks like the shape of Texas.

Yesterday there was no knock on the door. Nawaz looked preoccupied and distracted when he served us lunch. Tahira Aunty was in a crabby mood and barking more orders than usual at the poor boy. When she asked him to bring a plate of mangoes for desert, he accidentally brought the *kheer,* the rice pudding from last night's dinner and Tahira Aunty swore under her breath and said some nasty things in English right in front of Nawaz. She did this thinking that he couldn't understand her, but the wounded look in his eyes was ample evidence that he did. The whole incident prevented me from enjoying the mangoes which were *Anwar Ratole,* the choicest variety at their juiciest peak. Then Tahira Aunty and Rafiq Uncle started bickering and she chastised him for going to the bank without his cane when he should have been resting at home with his bad knee.

"One of these days, you're going to get hit by a bus. They're all maniacs. They don't look out for pedestrians."

"Then you'll become a widow. I dare say you'll be happier!"

As Nawaz was clearing up the table, he knocked over my glass of water. Tahira Aunty went ballistic.

"You clumsy oaf! Why can't you be more careful?"

"Leave him alone," Rafiq Uncle retorted. "He didn't do it on purpose."

Tahira Aunty went to her room in a huff. We could hear the television show she had turned on. Some chef was making a salad of grilled scallops on a bed of roasted fennel. Rafiq Uncle polished off the mangoes and asked for more just for spite because his wife won't let him eat too many sweets.

Back in my own room after lunch, I rummage through my contact list and unearth the number given to me by Bushra, one of my roommates back in Islamabad. It belongs to her cousin and when I call her up, she promptly invites me to go shopping in the evening. We plan for her to pick me up at the house at six. I take a nap, then shower and dress for my night on the town. Tahira Aunty does not look too happy, probably because I'm making her look bad as a host by making all my own arrangements. But I can't just sit around wasting precious time. I have yet to start building my wardrobe of chic Pakistani clothes. Lahore is known for some of the best, cutting edge trends. Bushra's cousin better be as fashion forward.

She has come with her mom and together the two of them look like sisters. We go to *Ichra,* the old bazaar with its cluttered lanes and bargain hard vendors that Bushra had talked about. I fall in love with a raw silk cloth with a delicate floral pattern in shades of aqua blue and tea rose. The shopkeeper knows I'm head over heels gaga and jacks up the price. I don't care to bargain. I have to have it. It will make for a gorgeous *lengha*, with a nice full skirt. My escorts take me to a back alleyway lined with small open air stalls where men are doing machine embroidery. You can choose a design from the ready outfits hanging on hooks which they will replicate on your fabric of choice. I settle on a bold geometric pattern that will be embroidered in thick black thread on a tunic of lime green crushed silk. A teenage boy takes my measurements. There is some dispute over the inseam length. I tell him to keep it shorter so the pants will look like capris. They will have it ready within a week. I get a hand written receipt scribbled in Urdu.

Afterwards, we go to a more modern part of Lahore to have dinner at McDonalds. I haven't had a cheese burger for ages and it tastes sinfully delicious. The mother and daughter duo treats me with cordial politeness, but I sense their reserve that keeps our conversation at the level of small talk. I miss the warmth of Beenish and her blabber mouth mother and that eventful weekend in Mansehra. I even miss Adam Khan and his volcanic flare-ups. They were all so full of passion.

*   *   *

"There is an old Punjabi saying. He who has not seen Lahore has not lived."

Rafiq Uncle raises his hand to silence my rebuttal.

"I know all too well what you're going to say, my Dear. We have been a little too protective of you. Quite so. Quite so. But it's just Tahira's way of being affectionate. She's really quite fond of you, you know."

I remind Rafiq Uncle ever so gently that I'm not a complete novice when it comes to travel.

"Yes, yes, I've heard," he responds. "It's rather unusual for Pakistani girls to be so footloose. Most of them would like nothing better than to be wined and dined at the gymkhana and attending fancy parties."

Rafiq Uncle glances at my frayed jeans and wrinkled *kurta*. "You don't look like the gymkhana type. Bird of a different feather, eh?"

"Aunty doesn't see me as Pakistani," I respond defensively. "She thinks I'm 100% American."

Rafiq Uncle chuckles.

"Oh don't let her get to you! My wife can be very black and white in her thinking. It is hard for her to see all the gray matter in between."

"And I'm that gray matter?"

"The very personification of it!"

Rafiq Uncle pats me on the head in a there there gesture.

"Don't look so glum. We'll get something sorted out worthy of your Marco Polo ambitions."

I manage a smile.

"I'll see what I can do," Rafiq Uncle adds with a wink.

He sits in the garden all evening and reads his paper. I go back to my room planning to take a shower and get some work done before dinner. But soon I've fallen asleep amid a pile of newspaper cuttings and hand written notes. I dream about a horse galloping across the desert. There appears to be no rider. Or perhaps he is invisible, a phantom in the sand dunes.

When I wake up, my watch reads nine thirty PM. I've missed dinner, but I go down just the same to get some leftovers. The table has been cleared and the kitchen is spotless with the lights turned off. Nawaz must have taken a night off. Either that or he has run off to one of his friends in the local bazaar to sample some homemade *daroo*, the poor man's moonshine. I open the fridge looking for some of Nawaz's excellent chicken chow mien from the night before and accidentally knock over a pitcher of orange juice. It shatters all over the floor which is now sticky and sweet. I find a wet rag and dab it on the mess cursing my clumsiness. One more mark against me in Tahira Aunty's book.

"We're in here!"

Her shrill voice beckons from the bedroom. I knock briefly before opening the door and find the mistress of the house curled up on her bed watching yet another cooking show featuring an Italian chef. She has company tonight. A petite woman with a café au lait complexion, frizzy short hair and horn rimmed glasses. Tahira Aunty introduces me to her older sister who also lives in Lahore, in the newer development known as Garden City. I was not aware of a sibling. Tahira Aunty's attention seeking mannerisms made me presume that she was an only child. The sister looks at me and smiles warmly. They don't look the least bit alike.

"Sorry about dinner. I overslept."

"It's quite alright, my dear. You must have needed the rest. Your face has been looking so haggard lately."

Her sister gives us a questioning look.

"She's a writer," Tahira Aunty responds. "From Boston."

I don't bother to amend it. Boston. Seattle. It's all the same to her. Besides, as far as she's concerned, I'm just a spoiled American brat who has no respect for her elders.

"Come sit with us."

The sister pats her side of the bed. I prop myself on the edge and eye a plate of cashews on the nightstand. No I musn't. If I touch just one, I won't be able to stop.

"He's making tiramisu!"

Tahira Aunty leans forward, hands on both knees with her gaze fixated at the television screen. I don't know what it is with her and cooking shows. She's not much of a chef herself, not even an aspiring one having relegated all the cooking duties of her household to Nawaz. It's unlikely that Tahira Aunty even knows how to boil an egg. Yet here she is fascinated with the eggy concoction the Italian guy is pouring onto the lady fingers. Maybe it's a fantasy thing, a taste for living vicariously where everything is at a safe distance, food, people, places. The very thought of it depresses me.

"How is your research coming along?"

"Pretty good. I have most of the data now. I'll finish up my report when I get back to the States."

Tahira Aunty looks disappointed. I know she's clamoring for a second meeting with I.A. Rehman to make a more favorable impression, but there will be no need for it. The HRCP director wasn't a stickler about deadlines. He wished me well on my journey and told me to send my write up on the Hudood laws whenever it was ready. The arrangement suited me just fine.

We hear a low droning sound like a chopper in mid-flight. It turns out to be the sister who has fallen asleep on the bed snoring.

"Poor old thing," Tahira Aunty says and covers her with a shawl. "She's had so much to deal with her husband's illness."

She nods towards my questioning gaze and divulges some details in her characteristic blunt way. "He's got a tumor. Only a matter of time."

"I'm so sorry."

"Yes, well, no point in dwelling over the matter. It's out of our hands."

She must not have liked the guy very much. The sister has stopped snoring. Her small body is curled up into a fetal position. I wonder what kind of life she has known. From what little Tahira Aunty had told me about herself, I learned that she had fled the partition riots in what would soon become an independent India by boarding a train in the direction of Lahore. She was one of the lucky ones who had survived the journey. To give herself immunity, she had taken on a Christian name passing herself off as Anglo-Indian with her fair skin. Tahira Aunty knew some Hail Marys from her Catholic school upbringing where she had also sang hymns in the all girls choir. The irony was revealing. A Muslim pretending to be a Christian to prevent getting massacred by Hindus. It was under these circumstances that Pakistan was born.

And this is why the Pakistani in me bears conflict like a coat of arms. And no matter where in the world I go, no matter how far removed my life might become from the country of my origins, somehow, somewhere, I will be reminded of this conflict, even though it has become something which I no longer wish to decipher, nor articulate, to unsuspecting strangers, even to myself, because the words are simply not there anymore to imprint the measure of pain, the wound so deep that it has become bottomless.

But still it flares up from time to time, like when my brother was denied a visa for his business trip to India on account of his Pakistani birth. The Indian authorities did not care for the fact that brother is an American citizen and Vice President of his company. It was just that one line on his U.S. passport that rattled their pea sized brains.

Place of Birth: Karachi, Pakistan.

It hadn't yet happened to me only because I hadn't been back to India since 1990. My brother was traveling in the post 9/11 era when the world as we know it has changed forever. Who knows what would happen if they gave him permission to fly into Delhi. He might be the next shoe bomber or an undercover Al-Qaeda agent, posing as a marketing consultant to do some shady dealings.

"Why don't you come by the school tomorrow?"

Tahira Aunty's voice breaks my train of thoughts. I'm still in her bedroom and it is nearly midnight now and my grumbling stomach is reminding me that I haven't eaten a thing in the last eight hours. The plate of cashews is still there. I can no longer resist.

"Yeah, sure, I'd love to."

"Good! It's settled then. We will leave first thing in the morning at seven thirty. If you're late, I shall go on without you."

"I wouldn't dream of missing it."

"I should hope not, my dear! It will be good for you to come see our education system. So much more evolved than those dreadful public schools you've attended in America. You ought to see what you've missed out on. And there's no need for that smug grin, young lady!"

Her remarks are hurtful and I'm too tired to argue with Tahira Aunty. So I take my leave and go back to my room to collapse in bed. My mind is swimming with thoughts as I drift in and out of sleep. Tahira Aunty has got it all wrong again, forgetting about my Mama Parsi years in Karachi. It may seem odd that I had gone to a Zoroastrian school as a Muslim. But it was known as one of the best private schools for girls in Karachi. I was at that school until the fifth grade. My favorite subject was Elocution where we learned poetry by rote and I still have on my bookshelf more than twenty five years later a hefty volume entitled the English Book of Verse filled with the classics.

When it came time to tell my classmates that I was leaving Pakistan for America, it was right in the middle of my final year's exams and I was already a nervous eleven year old trying to memorize everything from Blake to Wordsworth to T.S. Elliot. On the day of the exam, I had to put my hand inside a glass jar and draw out a slip of paper with the name of the poem to be recited in front of the class. Giggles erupted from all corners of the classroom when I fumbled the verses of *Tiger, Tiger*.

Only Sabahat, my best friend since kindergarten, had remained silent, offering an encouraging smile as I repeated the opening stanza.

Tiger Tiger, burning bright, in the forests of the night,
What immortal hand or eye dare frame thy fearful symmetry?
Blake. My beloved Blake. How I had missed him over the years.
He was nowhere in the picture in my next school, in the suburbs of
Seattle. My homeroom teacher, Mr. Rhoades, wore fraying jeans with
an old letterman jacket and allowed all sorts of liberties amongst his
students who chewed bubble gum while slouching in their chairs
and blurted out questions without raising their hands, all of which I
found rather strange and magical. I relished the freedom to be able to
wear whatever I wanted to school after all those years in that Mama
Parsi uniform with the sky blue tie and polished black shoes. My
new American uniform consisted mostly of Levi's and sweatshirts. I
joined the track team and took Spanish as my foreign language.

It was only during roll call when all my strides in cultural
assimilation came to a sickening halt. My heart started beating just a
little bit faster and I squirmed my feet and longed to melt into the floor
as soon as the teacher made it midway through the alphabet, slowly
moving past the K's and L's toward the M's. I knew just when that
pause would arrive, a nondescript five seconds that seemed like five
hours. And then, like a badly aimed slingshot, my name flew from
the teacher's mouth, polysyllables laced together in odd combinations
or sometimes missing vital components as in the case of Mali.

That mangled mispronunciation of Maliha reminded me of what
I was attempting to forget, of what was unforgettable. I was still a
girl from Karachi and that would never change. In those days,
whenever I told my friends and teachers that I was from Pakistan,
their faces went completely blank. They were all are clueless about
the country despite what was happening on the international stage
in the early 1980's when Pakistan became a crucial player in America's
proxy war in Afghanistan. My gym teacher thought Pakistan might
be a small colony in Africa. I didn't know whether to laugh or cry.

That night I have another strange dream. I am eight or nine years
old and playing lacrosse in a wide open field. But instead of hitting
the ball, I'm batting at something that hangs from a tree branch. It
looks like a Mexican piñata shaped like a camel. My aim is bad and
the camel piñata keeps swinging away. I try again and again. Then I
see my father watching me from the sidelines. He is wearing a dunce

cap and making silly faces. Then he disappears and standing in his place is General Zia in his walrus mustache and oil slicked hair parted down the middle. The General is waving his hands back and forth like a conductor. The camel piñata bursts open and I'm showered with snowflakes. Then I see nothing else except whiteness. A blizzard. I wake up in a start my legs thrashing.

A sliver of bright sunlight peaks into my room from the partially drawn curtains. I fumble around for my glasses and grab the digital travel alarm clock on my nightstand. It reads 9:30 AM. Great. I've missed my appointment with Tahira Aunty. She must really have it in for me now. Rafiq Uncle is still at the breakfast table when I venture downstairs reading his newspaper. He wipes off some crumbs from the corner of his mouth with a cloth napkin and gives me a big smile.

"I have a surprise for you!"

"Oh yes?"

"Tahira and I talked it over in the morning. Yes, yes, I know you were planning on going to school with her, but she let you sleep in because I've made some other arrangements for you today."

"What kind of arrangements?"

"You're going to see the old city. The fort, the *masjid*, the bazaar, the works!"

I clap my hands with glee.

"Nawaz will take you. I've given him the day off. He knows Lahore very well. Don't worry. Tahira and I have already discussed it. You must see these places before you go. We wouldn't have it any other way."

"Thank you. Thank you so much."

I try to contain my excitement, but my heart is not listening. It's doing all kinds of flip flops and somersaults. A tourist! I'm going to be a tourist. It's about time. Oh, is it ever.

"You can easily take in the main sights this afternoon. And tomorrow you can go to see the Khewra Salt Mines up north. Plenty of history and nature galore. Just your cup of tea, eh?"

"Sounds great!"

"Good! Off you go then. Now where's that boy gone? Nawaz! Oh Nawaz!!"

*   *   *

To walk though Lahore's fortified palace complex or *Shahi Qilla* as it is known in Urdu is to feel the grandeur of empire. Construction began in the mid sixteenth century when Lahore was briefly the capital of the Mughal dynasty in India under the Emperor Akbar. The palace was later expanded and modified by a continuous line of noble successors, from Jehangir to Shah Jehan and Aurangzeb. Our approach is from the main gate known as the *Alamgiri Darwaza* on the eastern rim of the fort that leads up a sharply angled passageway, to the large courtyard of the *Diwan-i-Amm,* the hall of the people, where the emperor's subjects would assemble a town hall meeting to voice their concerns and grievances and petition for favors.

Nawaz points out the huge archway that was designed to allow the emperor's elephant mounted caravan to pass through. The *Hathi Paer* or Elephant Path is a staircase consisting of fifty eight low and broad stone slabs built for the lumbering gray beasts. Some of the walls are scarred by bullet marks. We make our way to the northwest corner towards the fort's *Sheesh Mahal* most famous for being featured in the blockbuster Indian epic *Mughal-e-Azam.* There is a fantastic movie scene in which the shimmering, dizzying palace of mirrors comes to glorious Technicolor life as the beautiful courtesan Anarkali dances for the prince in the Emperor's court singing *Pyar Kiya to Darna Kya,* translating as I have loved, so what is there to fear?

Madhubala, the Muslim actress playing the role of Anarkali was one of the most sought after screen sirens of 1950's Indian cinema. She was even courted by Hollywood producers who saw her as a beautiful and mysterious woman of the East with a humungous fan base. The American magazine *Theatre Arts* did a feature article on Madhubala in their August 1952 issue entitled *The Biggest Star in the World (And She's Not in Beverly Hills).* It featured a glamorous full page shot of Madhubala looking every bit as compelling as Rita Hayworth or Betty Davis. The article hadn't mentioned anything about Madhubala's Islamic background. Why bother pointing out that an Indian movie star happened to be a Muslim? But, like it or not, Madhubala was living proof of Muslim womanhood, Indian Muslim womanhood as being sexy and smart.

She was born on Valentine's Day in 1933 in the city of Peshawar which ought to make Madhubala Pakistani rather than Indian, in a strictly geographical sense, even though there was no such thing as Pakistan at the time and the Northwest Frontier region was part of British India, which would mean that Madhubala was a onetime colonial subject. But it's far simpler to think of her as an icon of India which she undoubtedly was and always will be. For what it's worth, *Mughal-e-Azam* was one of the top grossing films in Indian film history. The story is set during the height of Islam's major ruling dynasties, its characters and flavors and textures are thoroughly Muslim, its lead actress was Muslim and yet one thinks of the film as Indian through and through, a nostalgic product of Bollywood, where even today, some of the biggest stars happen to be Muslim. It's a fact that goes unmentioned, unnoticed because there is no shock value or fear factor to be exploited.

Unfortunately, the *Sheesh Mahal* is closed for renovation work. As I walk past the scaffolding, I recall once again that unforgettable dance scene with the vixen (go ahead, folks, preface it with Muslim if you dare) twirling and pouting and seducing her beloved inside the palatial chamber decorated with hundreds of tiny, intricate mirrors, the whole effect being that of a star studded universe. Incidentally, the *Sheesh Mahal's* original purpose was not to be a setting for parties and festivities and movie crews, as much as for official business matters between the Emperor and his entourage of advisors. According to my guidebook, this part of Lahore's fort has been declared a UNESCO World Heritage Site since 1981.

Nawaz draws my attention to another nearby building, a rather unique structure also in white marble with a curvy rooftop. We walk inside the *Naulakha* Pavilion overlooking a panoramic view of the old city. Nawaz snaps a few pictures of me framed in an archway. I want to take a shot of him as well, but he is too camera shy. We discuss instead the meaning of *Naulakha* which Nawaz says is Urdu for nine *lakh*, the apparent cost of this structure, an exorbitant amount equaling 900,000 Rupees. Maybe that's why the Mughal Dynasty did not last more than two hundred years. The Emperors must have gone bankrupt funding all this magnificent architecture. By the mid-eighteenth century, their power considerably weakened amidst a period of infighting and outside attacks that paved the way for the British, who had already established business interests in India's southern and western regions, to seize more and more territory and eventually replace one empire with another.

It is mid afternoon and blazingly hot by the time we cross over from the fort to the Badshahi mosque. Nawaz has taken off his sandals and urges me to do the same as he walks barefoot on the smooth red flagstones of the mosque's immense courtyard reputed to be the largest in the world. I yowl with pain as my feet make contact with the sun baked floor. It's a red hot fire. Nawaz does not even flinch. He is waiting for me by the entrance of the main prayer hall, dwarfed by the mosque's sheer size and scale. Built under the reign of the austere minded Aurangzeb, the Badshahi appears as an ultra feminine bride wearing modest shades of dusky rose and mauve. All around us are rich embellishments in stucco and marble inlay.

People wander in and out of the seven large compartments. Local Punjabi families, Muslim tourists from Indonesia, Malaysia, Iran and various parts of Africa as well as a smattering of foreign backpackers in T-shirts and stringy blond hair. My eyes are drawn to all the men huddled against the walls, sleeping in the mosque's cool shade with their faces partially covered with cloth. Some of them may be homeless. Others may not have much of a home to retreat to.

We trudge deeper into the streets of old Lahore amid whirls of dust, crowds and noise. It feels as though a museum has come to life singing about its concealed treasures. Nawaz strides ahead and keeps turning his head to make sure I'm still following. I keep losing sight of him because of all my photo shoots of the crumbling windowed facades above the shops, intricately carved in wood. There are all manners of things on sale in the bazaar. Aluminum pots and pans. Terra cotta *matkas* and bowls. Ropes and mouthpiece attachments for water pipes. Great big bunches of loofah mitts and scrubbers. Spices in cones of green, brown, ochre, orange and red. Shimmering glass bangles. Fruit carts laden with finger length bananas that are weighed on a hand scale counterweighed by small cast iron tablets.

I try to be extra vigilant and observant while trying not to get run over by rickshaws and motorbikes carousing mere inches from my feet. A group of eunuchs, known throughout South Asia as *hijras,* beckon me to sample their *paan*. They smear some leaves with red paste and white lime, adding betel nuts and a pinch of chewing tobacco and fold the entire thing like a burrito. When I refuse and keep on walking, they circle around me, jeering and taunting. Nawaz tells me to accept the *paan*, otherwise I shall be the subject of a *hijra*'s curse which could spell a bad omen for the rest of my journey.

One of the *hijras* saddles up to me and strokes my hair. I am clearly being cajoled and hoodwinked and have no way out other than to give into their charade. The *paan* has a pleasant sweetness that cuts through the tart juices which one spits out on the streets. It's a pretty horrific sight that could easily be mistaken for blood gushing from the *paan* chewer's mouth. I choose to maintain some decorum and do my spitting in a wad of Kleenex.

When a small neighborhood mosque known as Wazir Khan comes into view, I immediately turn towards the entrance. Two men follow me into the courtyard insisting on a tour. I tell them in Urdu that I am not a tourist and only wish to pray. They eye my bulging camera and demand money. I suspect they are not official guides and only loitering around the mosque to harass foreign visitors, most of whom only make it to the more famous Badshahi that is the complete opposite of this intimately scaled structure. The men pull back as Nawaz approaches, but they still keep staring as though they have nothing better to do.

I fork over fifty Rupees to get rid of them. Now they are breaking into grins and bidding me *salaam,* farewell the old-fashioned way, hands touching forehead and swinging down to the waist and repeating the gesture in a fluid arc, five to six times while walking backwards. I am tempted to snap their picture, but turn on my heels and head towards a faucet to wash up.

As I place my shawl on the cool marble floor and turn towards Mecca, I am peeved to find a small audience of young boys has gathered on the ramparts to watch my performance. Never mind. Let them watch. It's not every day one gets to be the star attraction in a place of worship. After prayers, I wander around what seems to be the architectural equivalent of a Persian carpet.

The tile work is exquisite with colors that look good enough to eat. Lemon bisque, rose sherbet, pomegranate red, mint green, golden pumpkin. I keep my *dupatta* wrapped over my head. It feels like a cozy cocoon. There is something about this place that makes me want to linger all evening. A feeling of spirituality over holiness. The sky turns pink and lavender. Soon it will be dusk. I see Nawaz in the distance wandering about the mosque on his own sensing my need for some solitude. No other visitors have showed up.

An old woman guards the pavilion in the courtyard which is a saint's tomb. She is lighting candles as we pass by. Nawaz slips her a hundred Rupee note that I offer as a small tip to the universe for keeping me safe on this journey. So much could have gone wrong. So much did go wrong. But I've been tremendously lucky to have suffered no serious harm. Someone has been keeping watch.

Back in the bazaar, Nawaz leads me through a narrow alleyway. I hear the sound of women's voices singing. Large green banners hang from the sides of balconies and windows. A young girl's face peaks out of a doorway decorated with a silver tinsel fringed curtain. The voices get louder and more melancholic. I stand underneath a window and listen to the *marsiahs,* Shia lamentations mourning the death of the prophet's grandsons. The women's voices are getting downright frightening now. At one point, they sound like a medley of dying cats.

My mind flashes back to the Shia procession during the month of *Muharram* that passed by our Saddar house in Karachi. Mistri was my family's all around gofer, errand boy and loyal servant. He would prop me up on the concrete wall surrounding our bungalow and together we would sit, feasting on sticky *jelabis* as hordes of men naked from the waist up shouted *Ya Ali, Ya Ali* while whipping themselves with knives and various sharp instruments. Blood trickled down bare brown backs. Blood flew in my direction and decorated my *kurta* in bright red splotches. The men continued their passion play as though they were in a trance. Instead of being terrified, I was fascinated by their actions, by the intensity and conviction of a belief system that led to such drama. It was more than just a senseless exercise in self-flagellation. It was a tribute to the past, because the past does live on in our skin and our bones--and no matter what the times dictate--the past is our blueprint, an indelible cheat sheet of who we are.

*   *   *

"Teekh se pakro."

Hold on properly. I readjust my grip on Nawaz's shoulders as his motorcycle zips along the GT road. We are heading to the Wagah border between Pakistan and India which is about half an hour away. The road that we're on connects two major nations that were formerly one and before that several. It is one of the great thoroughfares of the subcontinent, forming a continuous link stretching from Calcutta across the Northern plains of India all the way up to Peshawar and through the Khyber Pass to the Afghan border, a distance of about sixteen hundred miles.

If there could be a Muse for the road, then the Grand Trunk Road would most certainly qualify. Its American counterpart would be the Oregon Trail, the Appalachian Trail and Route 66 all rolled up in one scenic byway rich in history and diversity. What I like best about the GT road is how it brazenly mocks politics and the quirks of geography, defiantly getting on with the more practical matters of transportation.

We have just crossed a bridge over the Ravi River, also known as the river of Lahore given the city's location on its eastern bank. As if the physical separation of India and Pakistan had not created enough chaos and conflict, the problem was compounded by the vagaries of partition that overlooked the issue that rivers emptying into Pakistan originated in India. Water sharing has remained a cantankerous battle ground resolved interminably by treaties such as the Indus Waters Treaty designed to safeguard Pakistan's potential for drought and famine especially during times of war with its arch rival and nemesis next door.

There is a loud thud and the bike starts to wobble out of control. We have hit a piece of metal and punctured a tire. Nawaz wheels the bike to the nearest auto repair shop as I walk alongside a steady stream of traffic. People are gaping at us, but I don't care. I look straight ahead, my gait as sure footed as possible in a pair of flimsy sandals tottering along the GT road. We approach a dirt lot with some crowbars and lots of inner tubes. It must be the auto shop. A young boy takes charge of the motorcycle while another one brings us some tea. I take a seat on a plastic chair and plant myself in the middle of the open lot so everyone can gape at the crazy foreigner and have a good laugh. While I wait, an old man drags his charpoy next to me and shares some orange slices dabbed in salt.

Nawaz is hunched over his bike watching the boy fix the tire. It takes him about fifteen minutes to finish the job. There is a small dispute since Nawaz doesn't have enough money for the repair. An older man comes over and exchanges some harsh words with the boy mechanic and then pushes him roughly by the shoulder in a gesture of disapproval. I hand over a hundred rupee note as a peace offering. Nawaz looks at me with gratitude and wipes his sweaty brow. We decide to hold off the trip to Wagah for another time.

The following day we set out for a more ambitious excursion leaving Lahore by six thirty in the morning heading via Daewoo to Islamabad, from where we will make our way south to the Salt Range. Nawaz wanted to skip the whole luxury coach passage to Isloo and go straight to Chakwal, the largest town in the area. It was only a matter of taking half a dozen or more local minivans--most of them rundown and packed from floor to ceiling--and then finding some other manner of vehicular means to take us to the mines. He did not specify the details and I didn't bother to ask, having long ago given up any semblance of exactitude when it comes to traveling in Pakistan via public transport. What you gain in adventure is usually worth the effort, provided you have ample tolerance and a good sense of humor. I've started to run low on both reserves which is why we have opted for the convenience and roomy air conditioned comfort of Pakistan's preeminent private bus company.

It feels good to be out and about so early in the morning. The streets are mellower with people simply milling about getting their day started. Our bus is on schedule and getting fuller by the minute as we board. No one seems to care that Nawaz and I are sitting next to each other and though I'm glad to be left alone for once and spared the hassles of horny drivers rubbing against my thighs and conductors encroaching on my personal space and telling me where I can and cannot be seated, I also vaguely miss all that *hungama*, the noise and commotion of those rickety buses that had taken me to Mansehra with Beenish's mother and brother, who were servants just like Nawaz, but unlike Nawaz, not as lucky to be given their own private room next to a rooftop terrace with adjoining bath and access to hot running water. Even among servants, there are layers of distinction separating the haves from the have nots.

"Juice?"

Nawaz hands me a small carton of mango nectar loaded with sugar. It quenches my thirst better than water so I drink carton after carton, not caring what they might do to my waistline. A flimsy plastic bag tucked under Nawaz's feet holds all our food provisions. He is all spiffed up for the outing in polished new shoes that look like penny loafers. Instead of his usual faded blue jeans, he is wearing a pair of black ones with a thicker fabric. They are paired with a simple white oxford type shirt with the sleeves carefully rolled up to the elbows. The overall effect is chic and preppy like J.Crew and I can't help but wonder where Nawaz got his sense of style.

What a relief it must be for him to escape for the day from all of Tahira Aunty's orders and commands. At least she has given us the latitude to team up as a travel party for which I'm tremendously grateful. It's not like me to shirk from intrepid exploration, but I don't have the fortitude in these waning days of the journey to be roughing it on the road and traipsing off solo to see some Pakistani salt mines. The only reason I'm going is because Nawaz is by my side.

But it all starts to go downhill the minute we reach Islamabad.

There are no direct bus services to the Salt Range. We are advised to go to the Punjabi town of Jhelum on the banks of the Jhelum River and pick up local transport bound for Chakwal. Alternatively, we could go to Mandra, just south of the Islamabad-Lahore Motorway and take a minivan that runs frequently on the road running parallel to the railway. There used to be a train service from Mandra to Chakwal, but it is now closed. I'm starting to get a colossal headache. Nawaz remains upbeat and cheerful. He has the patience and stamina to withstand this shuttling around from town to town, for walking along busy roadsides with no pavement or shoulder and waiting at hot dusty stations for buses that may or may not come, but I most certainly don't, at least not anymore.

If this were my very first excursion in Pakistan and had I newly arrived in the country in that honeymoon stage when everything appears so wonderfully new and exciting and ripe for discovery, I would have been all for it, my openness and enthusiasm for the unknowns along the way greatly outweighing any misgivings or apprehensions of what could go wrong. A person can change a lot in the course of five months.

At this point, I am not the least bit inclined to go to Jhelum or Mandra or any other wasteland that is not a straight shot to Khewra. There is only one viable option and though it's not the most economical, I won't settle for anything less than a taxi. We flag one down and by a stroke of good luck the driver appears sane and negotiates a sensible fee. The M2 highway cuts straight through the Salt Range and we're there within an hour and a half. The cabbie turns off his meter and decides to accompany us on the tour.

"Welcome, welcome!"

A portly middle aged man at the ticket counter greets us. He looks at me with interest and haphazardly attempts to answer his query.

"Egypt? Morocco? Turkey? Iran?"

"Karachi."

He looks disappointed and I march ahead sweeping my fallen *dupatta* back up to my shoulders in a hurried gesture that makes Nawaz laugh. While we wait for the train that will take us into the mines, I brush up on some background in my dog eared guidebook. Khewra happens to be the largest salt mine in the world in terms of area covering over two hundred and fifty square kilometers of which only a tiny fraction has so far been mined. It has had some illustrious visitors, such as Alexander the Great who came here to extract salt back in 327 BC. The use of steam engines during British rule has blackened some of the salt in the tunnels. The mine employs over two thousand salt cutters to produce some six hundred tons of salt per day.

The train takes us inside one of the tunnels to a small section at ground level where mining has been discontinued. I'm fascinated with the sculptural beauty of salt stalactites and stalagmites that remind me so much of the caves I had visited in France, Spain and Lebanon. Nawaz gravitates toward a glowing structure that turns out to be a small mosque inside the mine. Light trapped within its salt brick walls creates the glow in the dark effect in shades of pink, yellow and orange. I snap a picture of Nawaz and the taxi driver standing inside a chamber mined entirely by hand. My fingers scrape against the rough walls engraved with the chiseler's lines. The taxi driver hands me a chunk of salt rock that looks like crystal. I slip it inside my *kurta's* pocket for a lasting keepsake.

As we board the train to go back outside, it gets rowdy with a group of Pakistani high school kids. They have kilowatts of energy to burn and their raging hormones keep them hooting and shouting at each other. Their speech is a peculiar mix of Americanized English and Urdu flagrant with *arre yaar* as in oh you guys and the ever present Ohmygosh and no ways. Is this how I would have turned out had I never left the country I wonder for the umpteenth time. Everyone waves boisterous goodbyes as the train ride ends. Some of the feistier kids stick out their tongues.

Nawaz and I head towards the waiting taxi. The portly ticket collector runs after us with offerings of chai. We politely decline. It is nearly dusk and I'm anxious to get back home to Aunty before she calls the police to track us down. The cabbie drops us right outside the Daewoo station in Islamabad where the passenger lounge is eerily empty. I dine on soggy *aloo parathas* on the ride back to Lahore.

*   *   *

Not all the inmates were insane. Quite a few were murderers. To escape the gallows, their relatives had gotten them in by bribing the officials. They had only a vague idea about the division of India or what Pakistan was. They were utterly ignorant of the present situation. Newspapers hardly ever gave the true picture and the asylum warders were illiterates from whose conversation they could not glean anything. All that these inmates knew was that there was a man by the name of Quaid-e-Azam who had set up a separate state for Muslims, called Pakistan. But they had no idea where Pakistan was. That was why they were all at a loss whether they were now in India or in Pakistan. If they were in India, then where was Pakistan? If they were in Pakistan, how come that only a short while ago they were in India?

How could they be in India a short while ago and now suddenly in Pakistan? One of the lunatics got so bewildered with this India-Pakistan-Pakistan-India rigmarole that one day while sweeping the floor he climbed up a tree, and sitting on a branch, harangued the people below for two hours on end about the delicate problems of India and Pakistan. When the guards asked him to come down he climbed up still higher and said, "I don't want to live in India and Pakistan. I'm going to make my home right here on this tree."

And so goes the short story entitled *Toba Tek Singh* by Sadat Hasan Manto, in which an inmate in an asylum frets over the question of whether his home town Toba Tek Singh is in India or Pakistan. Towards the end, we find him at the Wagah border in Lahore where an exchange of lunatics is about to take place. The Muslim lunatics from India will cross into Pakistan. The Hindu and Sikh lunatics in Pakistan transfer to India. But Bishan Singh, the story's main character is resistant to the whole sordid operation.

Unable to ascertain the precise location of his village, he shrieks and collapses in a no-man's-void between the newly demarcated Indian and Pakistani barbed-wire posts. His dilemma remains unresolved. It is arguable that our conflicted hero might not belong to either India or Pakistan, being like me, an inextricable product of both countries. Or maybe his home lies right on the fault line, that senseless tear in the land that has no allegiance to any nation, but simply exists as it is, betwixt and between. We never really learn if he is sane or mad, conscious or delirious, alive or dead. With delicious subtlety and literary restraint, the author allows us to invent our own ending.

I've been contemplating it all morning sitting in bed with Manto's slim volume open in my lap. It is the copy that Tahira Aunty had given me when we first met at the airport upon my arrival in Lahore more than six weeks ago. I'm glad the book is an English translation as my Urdu is not nearly good enough to have deciphered the original text published in 1955, the same year as Manto's death. I had never read any of his work before, but I'm captivated by this story which I'd read last night on the bus. It is a brilliant piece of satire told with deadpan wit and one of the most powerful accounts of partition ever recorded in literature.

Manto's story has made me more agitated, my mood keeps swinging like a pendulum between sadness and anger, exhaustion and restlessness. I know that time in Lahore is fleeting, the journey almost drawing to a close, yet there is still so much more to explore, so much to think about, to reimagine, so much to dream and to live.

There is a knock at the door and then Nawaz pokes his head to announce lunch is ready. I had skipped breakfast too caught up with the book to bother about something as trivial as eating, but now I really am famished.

Khana! Food. My mouth salivates at the thought of Nawaz's *rotis*, maybe some of his *aloo gobi*, potato with cauliflower that he makes with tiny black cumin seeds known as *kalongee*.

Give me five minutes to get ready, I tell Nawaz. He wags his head from side to side and closes the door softly. I smile, thinking about our first awkward meeting when he had stood in the same doorway, his posture as still as a man that had been zapped by lightening. The rapport between us is friendlier now with him less intimidated by my status as the foreigner, the *mehman*, the guest from America, while I would sooner forget his status as a servant and treat him simply as a person, as Nawaz.

We've made a good travel team in spite of, or more likely, because of our innumerable differences, comfortable in the gaps between our chit chat, knowing instinctively when to leave the other alone with a natural easy going camaraderie that can take years to develop. Come to think of it, Nawaz has been one of the best travel partners I've ever had and that's saying a lot given my dogged preference for solo travel put to the test in all parts of the world, from Europe to the Middle East and now Pakistan.

I wish I could tell him all this, but the words don't come out since there are no words to express all these churned up feelings. The Toba Tek story continues to haunt my thoughts. Where, oh where, do I ultimately belong?

According to my return ticket, I have to fly out of Pakistan in ten days and resume my real life back in America. Just ten more days. Part of me wants to leave. The other half is not sure. I don't fancy sitting prisoner like in Aunty's gilded fortress in these precious few days. The excursions with Nawaz were just a onetime deal. Tahira Aunty needs him back in her kitchen. I'm on my own again. But no, not necessarily so. There's one other place I have to see. It's right here in the Punjab, the very heart of it, one of the oldest cities in Pakistan. Culture, history and architecture, it has it all and there is even someone I know there, or rather someone who knows someone who might be able to get me to this someone.

I dig out my contact book and find Anwar's number right on page one. The first time I had called him up he had shown me the Khyber Pass. After that, it was Peshawar. I just hope his wife Salma is at home. She's the one I need to talk to. The lady from Multan.

And Bingo, it's done. We haven't worked out too many details. Salma simply gives me her mother's home phone number in Multan. That's all the assurance I need. Of course, I'm counting on Salma to inform her *Ammijan* about the girl from America who used to live in Pakistan a very very very long time ago and who will be coming to stay with her for a few days and of course Salma's mother will say yes, for she is kind and hospitable like most Pakistanis and nothing would give her more pleasure than to host a total stranger in her home. Amen.

I practically skip my way downstairs.

"There she is! We thought you'd forgotten all about us."

Tahira Aunty pretends to pout. I can see right through the pretense, but at least the intent was good. She really seems to have missed me.

"Sorry, so sorry. I was caught up in some reading."

"It must have been bloody good stuff to keep you away from breakfast."

Rafiq Uncle looks up from his newspaper and smiles at me, the crinkles around his eyes somehow deeper and more prominent. I'm glad to see his face again. It's a face that I will always equate with Lahore.

"Toba Tek Singh."

"We'll talk about it later."

He gives me a knowing look as though he understands all too well that this is a subject that means a lot to me and maybe even to him, but it's not something to be rushed. We will get to it when the moment allows.

"I gather your excursions went well. I hope you're satisfied now."

I stifle a smile. It's so like Tahira Aunty to be gracious and stern at the same time. I will miss her blunt way of talking most of all. It gives her character.

"Yes, thank you. I enjoyed them very much."

"Good."

She takes some more rice and ladles some *daal* on top of it. Nawaz has outdone himself today. The *daal* is rich and velvety. He has made the rice Persian style, flavored with saffron with broken pieces of hardened crust decorating the pile.

"I'd like to see Multan," I say with my mouth full of food. "I've made arrangements to go there tomorrow."

"Oh?" Tahira Aunty raises her eyebrows. "And where will you be staying? Surely not in some dodgy guesthouse or third rate hotel. I absolutely forbid it. On no account are you going there only to get scammed..."

"I have an invitation to stay at a friend's house. Multan is her hometown. She's been there for ages. I'll be in good hands."

"Nonetheless, I shall still like her name, phone number and address."

"Sure."

Tahira Aunty sighs and carries on eating. She glances toward her husband who is busy dislodging something from his mouth with a toothpick.

"Don't forget to call us the minute you get there," she adds. "We shall sleep better knowing you've arrived in one piece and have a respectable roof over your head."

"Yes, of course. I wouldn't dream of doing otherwise."

"Multan, eh?" Rafiq Uncle murmurs. "City of dead saints. Have fun, my dear."

10

CITY OF DEAD SAINTS

Multan, September 2003

I HAD HALF A MIND TO GET THERE by rail, but in the interest
of time and comfort, I resort once more to my friends at Daewoo.
Tahira Aunty accompanies me with her chauffeur to the Lahore
station where we wait for the ten thirty morning connection for
Multan. It's a distance of about four hundred kilometers southwest
of Lahore and according to my printed bus ticket I will be there
precisely by four PM just when Tahira Aunty would be sitting down
with her third or fourth cup of sweet milky chai and watching the
usual marathon of cooking shows or yakking on the phone to her
son in Karachi or asking me how many channels one can get on cable
TV in America and which brand of food processor is the gold
standard, Cuisinart or KitchenAid.

I simply had to get away from all that. There is no better thrill than
being on my own again and navigating a brand new place amongst a
group of people who don't know me any better than a visiting alien.
Soon I'll be back on a jumbo jet fastening on my seat belt and watching
the stewardess demonstrating the use of an oxygen mask and pointing
to the aircraft's emergency exits prior to takeoff. Pakistan will become
just another distant memory, albeit something to hold onto and
treasure for the rest of my life.

It is cool and dark inside the bus with all the window shades
drawn to keep out the sun's glare. The seat adjacent to mine is empty

and there's only one other passenger across the aisle, a long legged teenage boy with huge ear muff style headphones glued to his Sony Discman. His knees are bouncing so hard that I'm afraid they're going to come loose at the sockets.

I busy myself with the *Daily Times*, a progressive English language Pakistani newspaper that has an interesting column about the concept of a constitution. It is written by Ejaz Haider, an acclaimed Pakistani journalist I had met in Boston when he came to speak at my school. He had offered me an ideal job writing a column for his paper from a Pakistani-American point of view. I could write about anything I wanted, so long as I spoke to both sides. It was a plum job, but I was too muddled at that point to think straight and failed to follow up. Nonetheless, we stayed in touch via emails planning to meet up again in DC where Ejaz was a visiting scholar at a prominent think tank. A few months later in January of 2003, Ejaz made international headlines when he was picked up on the streets of Washington by the US Immigration and Naturalization Service.

Whatever charges they brought up were eventually cleared, but Ejaz was pretty sore about the whole incident when I saw him shortly before leaving to spend my summer in Pakistan. I could understand his anger about the way he was treated like a common criminal and the inherent racism that had led to his arrest. But I could also see the need to be extra vigilant about national security when Americans were still reeling from the aftershocks of 9/11. What pains me is the knee jerk reaction of the arresting officers, their absolute inability to work around the presumption that all Pakistanis are dangerous and suspect. It is what it is.

"Madam! Madam! We're here!"

I wake up to the sensation of my shoulders being shaken. A pimply faced sophomore reeking of hair gel and wearing a T-shirt that says UCLA stands before me.

"Multan. Last stop."

It's Mr. Sony with headphones dangling around his neck. He looks concerned as though he's personally vouching for my safety. I don't feel like getting out of my seat. It's so plush and comfortable and I'm still drowsy and not at all in the mood to move. But move I must. The bus is empty now and a cleaning crew is picking up paper wrappers and sunflower seed husks carelessly strewn about.

I gather my belongings from the luggage rack and follow my newfound escort down the aisle. He stays by my side at the bus station as though I'm a lost puppy that needs looking after. I assure him that I'll be fine and demonstrate by taking out my address book to find the phone number that is my sole point of reference in this unknown town. I find a pay phone and dial. The boy has found his friend. They're knocking fists back and forth up and down in an elaborate greeting ceremony.

A woman's voice answers on the other line. Yes. Yes. She has been expecting me. Where am I? No problem. No problem. She will send her driver right away. Arshee will meet me. Her younger daughter. I am instructed to wait inside the station. She hangs up. A bit of a brusque attitude, but I don't dwell on it. I'm curious to see what this Arshee is like. Salma hadn't mentioned she had a sister.

They turn out to be complete opposites. While Salma was quiet and reserved, this sister of hers is a real firebrand. As soon as we meet, Arshee loops her arm into mine, winks like a trickster and pinches my cheeks with abandon. Then she ushers me into the back seat of a Land Rover and tells her driver to pump up the volume to the Bhangra music on the stereo. I feel as though we ought to be going to a club rather than her mom's house which is just off of Massoom Shah Road near the Stadium.

Arshee is going on and on about some incident at her farm to which I am only half listening. The passing scenery does not live up to Multan's reputation as an ancient dusty city bounding with burial grounds. The place looks thoroughly modern with billboards advertising bottled water, the ubiquitous Nestlé with its Urdu slogan *piyo aur jiyo* (drink and live), Coca Cola and TNT Worldwide Shipping. We even drive past a Pizza Hut and a Holiday Inn.

"And so I was just telling my husband the other day that he's been working too hard. He should spend more time at home with me, but the man might as well be deaf. I mean I know that he's the district *nazim* and all that. But I'm telling you, he's turned into a real work addict, just like you Americans. Work work work. That's all he thinks about. I might as well be married to a robot!"

Arshee tugs on my *dupatta* and whispers in my ear. The driver looks into his rear view mirror and our eyes meet as I double over with laughter at Arshee's crude joke that sex with her husband might as well be choreographed to the jack hammer pounding on the street. She starts to cackle hysterically and collapses her head on my shoulder. I take an instant liking to her easy warmth and wicked sense of humor.

Arshee speaks good English given her convent education and a degree from Punjab University. B.A in Psychology with honors Arshee proudly points out. Her family may be traditional, but they also have a steadfast tradition in educating their girls. It's their God given right as mentioned in the Quran. No Muslim should object to it and the ones that do are clueless about Islam.

Hear, hear. I silently applaud Arshee's sentiments. We are in total sync. She looks about my age and when I ask, she tells me she's thirty five and was married off at thirteen to her first cousin. Mopping her sweaty heart shaped face with the edge of her thin cotton *chador*, Arshee looks at me with the big brown eyes of a gazelle, her maroon painted mouth curving into a bewitching smile.

"So?"

"So what?"

"Are you married?"

"Not yet."

"Very good. Very good."

She pokes me in the ribs.

"Ouch! That hurts!"

"Sorry. Sorry."

"It's OK."

"Are you excited?"

"About what?"

"About getting married you silly girl!"

"I guess so. It's not something I've been thinking about a whole lot."

"Well you should start thinking about it. And soon! Otherwise you'll end up an old maid!"

"Don't say that. You're going to jinx everything."

"Jinx, what is this jinx?"

"It just means that you might spoil my luck by giving it the evil eye. You know, *nazar*."

"You really are very superstitious!"

"Can't help it. My Dadi's influence. She even thought the house she grew up in was haunted."

"And was it?"

"Yeah, maybe. They had all kinds of crazy stuff happen there."

"Well I don't doubt that. America is a crazy place, no?"

"I'm not talking about America. The house was in Madras."

"Madras? India?"

"Where else?"

"So you're Indian?"

"Technically no. But just between you and me, I have some, er, issues with Pakistan. Things are not as clear cut as they're made out to be."

"Oh, please, *yaar*! Let's not get into politics."

"Why not? It's all about politics."

"I, uhh, I don't do politics too well. I know. I know. I'm the wife of a *nazim*. I should be more learned about these things. But I really can't stand it. We don't have politics in Pakistan. We have one big circus!"

"Well said!"

The driver turns into a narrow side lane and stops by a thick stone wall about four feet tall. He opens a gate and pulls into the driveway. Arshee hooks arms again and escorts me towards the front door where a tall regal looking woman in an elegant navy colored *shalwar kameez* is smiling and nodding.

"*Asaalam Alaikum.*"

I offer the traditional Muslim greeting. Peace be upon you.

"*Walaikum as Salaam. Jeeti raho beeti.*"

And peace be upon you as well. Live long my child.

We give each other a hug. It would be rather stiff and formal and too foreign a gesture to shake hands.

"*Aao beeti aao.*"

The mother beckons me to come inside. I step into a large open room lined with mattress rolls and tin trunks. A flock of servants and children gather in a circle to inspect me from head to toe.

Arshee winks at me. I'm hoping she'll show me the ropes so I don't make too many awful blunders in this house, but right now she seems to be part of the audience simply watching me in the spotlight. We go into a smaller room which appears to be the mother's bedroom judging by the framed black and white wedding pictures on a dressing table with three paneled mirrors. Her eyes follow mine and she hands me one of the frames of a handsome young couple standing next to each other with solemn expressions. Arshee leans forward and wrinkles her nose.

"I don't like that one of her so much. My father looks good, but *Ammijan's* face is so morbid."

Arshee goes up to the dresser and pulls down another picture. "She's a real beauty queen in this one."

"Wow! What a gorgeous dress."

"That's one of my mother's hand made *lenghas*. She wanted me to wear it for my *shadi*, but I was too short for it. I don't know why she's still holding on to it. She should sell it in the bazaar and make some money out of it!"

"It's absolutely stunning."

"See *Ammijan*. She likes your *lengha*. Maybe you've found a customer!"

The mother smiles as though she's indulging a mischievous child which Arshee apparently still is.

"Aunty," I say as I hand her the framed picture. "You've got exquisite taste. Maybe you can take me shopping while I'm in Multan. I've heard so much about the local embroidery work. Salma told me to visit a famous bazaar in the old city. Hussain something. I forgot the name."

"Hussain Agahi. And no Aunty. Call me Najma."

"Najma."

We smile at each other politely.

A teenage boy comes in and sits down on the bed next to me staring as if he's seen a ghost. Najma barks a sharp order in Punjabi and he slinks off into a corner like a wounded dog, still staring.

"Don't mind him," Arshee says. "That's my idiot brother Faraj. He's a bit slow in the head, but don't let him get the better of you."

Najma barks another command this time to her daughter. Arshee winces and turns to me with a pensive expression.

"She's rather too protective of him. Our father died just before he was born. It's her big guilt trip. Not having any father figure around the house. She's had to do so much on her own."

"I'm very sorry."

"Oh, don't so glum! Let *Ammijan* take you to the bazaar. She's a real pro."

I don't want to prey on their generous hospitality any longer than I have already. But mother and daughter soon put their heads together and map out my entire itinerary for the next few days. Shopping tomorrow. Then a visit to the farm where Arshee lives. We should also go to her in laws village. A picnic or two if the weather cools down.

Now this is more like it. I had come to Multan for some much needed action and something tells me that I won't be disappointed.

* * *

It's one of the oldest parts of Multan. Ramshackle alleyways interspersed with mosques and the shops of tradesmen and artisans. We pass stalls selling grilled kabobs, blue and white glazed pottery and the psychedelic hues of a dye vendor.

"*Aao beti, aao.*"

Najma takes hold of my arm and gently pushes me through the bustling streets of the Hussain Agahi Bazaar. It combines all the intrigue of an ancient Arab *souq* with the boisterous hullabaloo of the subcontinent. The air is thick with the pungent smells of onions, incense, human and animal sweat. I stop to admire a pretty row of embroidered *khusa* shoes hanging in a doorway. Najma dissuades me from going in.

"*Lengha!*"

Najma steers me towards a large air conditioned shop where we sit on low stools and watch the salesman unfurl bolts of fabric. I select a burgundy georgette piece with an elaborate border of paisley and lotus blooms hand stitched in golden thread. The salesman tells me it's a traditional Rajasthani design from Northern India. Najma wants me to go with the turquoise taffeta topped with a transparent net, the latest style. I stay resolute in my choice. There's not much room to bargain and we settle on 3,500 Rupees, about seventy five dollars. It's an absolute steal. Najma offers to take me to her own tailor to get it stitched. Before I protest any further, we are back in her chauffeured car heading towards *Master-Jee.*

He turns out to be a three generation tailor outfitting Najma's long departed mother and now her and the two daughters. My measurements are taken on the spot and *Master-Jee* promises to have the *lengha* ready in a day or two so I can take it back with me to Lahore and eventually to America and wear it at some fancy shin dig.

"*Shukria.*"

Master-Jee dismisses my thanks with a gracious smile.

"*Aao, beti, aao.*"

I follow Najma as we stroll through the indoor shopping complex that is mostly a hodgepodge of fabric stores carrying the same merchandise, *dupattas* and *kurtas* embellished with Multani *karhai.* According to Najma, the local hand embroidered work is so fine and detailed that the village women laboring over it would have blood dripping from their fingers. She smiles with pride. I suspect the bloody fingers are a bit of an exaggeration as I haven't seen any such stains on her tasteful clothes. She is wearing purple today, a deep plum shade that complements her tawny complexion. Her head is partially covered with a sheer, off white *dupatta* loosely wrapped over the shoulders and chest in the manner of Benazir Bhutto. All in all, Najma is rather dashing for a woman in her mid fifties with far more style and confidence than the younger Pakistani girls I've seen in the cities with their fashion victim faux pas.

"*Idar chalo.*"

Come this way. Najma heads towards a row of jewelry shops and slips inside a stall glittering with gold. An exuberant looking older man with a sharply receding hairline appears behind the counter and I am introduced to Pir Jee. He is a family friend and according to Najma, somewhat of an amateur historian, specializing in the Mughal period.

"*Arre, hum to kuch naheen hain sevai insaan.*"

Don't pay any attention to her. I am simply a human being. Pir Jee dismisses Najma's repeated praise and twitches his nose. Najma says something that makes him laugh. They don't speak in Punjabi, which I can recognize without understanding, but in a completely different language. Pir Jee explains that it is Seraiki, classified as a branch of the Indo Aryan language like Urdu and one of the two major languages in this region of southern Punjab.

"Coke? Pepsi? Chai?"

"No thanks."

"*Kuch to lo, beti.*"

Najma insists that I have something, still referring to me by the endearing *beti* which translates as either daughter or child.

I settle on some chai, preferring something warm to quench my thirst because ice cold drinks in this tropical heat tend to give me a sore throat.

Pir Jee slides open a glass showcase and takes out a few sample pieces. I'm not a fan of gold which I find too gaudy when it comes to jewelry, but the matte gold is subtler and I choose a *tikka* with an oval pendant that will be worn in my hair and dangle over my forehead between the eyebrows. Najma urges me to take the matching necklace as well, a choker piece with filigree work set in small green synthetic stones made to look like malachite. It's a pretty set and I put it in the yes pile. Pir Jee offers to show me some silver. I take two more necklaces with matching earrings. He wraps up my purchases in small brown paper bags tied up with string and hands them to me with a big smile.

I have yet to pay him, but Pir Jee tells me not to worry about it. We can settle the bill later. No problem. No problem. He wobbles his head from side to side. It is nearly bald and reminds me of a half peeled egg. No other customers have shown up and I sense that Pir Jee is rather bored which is probably why he's so eager to talk. Pir Jee wishes there were more foreign tourists in Multan. He thinks most Pakistanis don't know or appreciate their own cultural heritage. He likens this to an inferiority complex vis a vis the West. I'm invited to a picnic the day after tomorrow. I immediately turn towards Najma, my trip coordinator in Multan who nods with approval. Good. Very good. Pir Jee rubs his palms with pleasure. It is all arranged. Someone from his family will pick me up at Najma's house. There will be a special guest. A visiting cousin. From America. I will be in good company.

On the way back, Najma and I stop at a shrine. It is the grave of Makhdum Syed Mohammad Yusuf Gardezi who had settled in Multan in the early 11ᵗʰ century. He was influential in converting much of the local population to Islam as well as being skilled at riding tigers and charming snakes. According to legend, his hand would occasionally slip out of his tomb for forty years after his death. The shrine is not as ostentatious as some of the more well known ones dotted around the fort. It is a simple rectangular building with no dome, but the tile work is exquisite. We sit down on the bare floor and take in the atmosphere. A small girl is selling rose petals to scatter on the saint's grave. Najma hands her a few rupees and asks me to do the honors.

I tell her that I don't believe in praying to saints or any of that *pir* worship nonsense which is a custom ingrained in much of South Asia.

I am not asking you to pray, she points out just as firmly. I am simply asking you to pay some respects, what's wrong with that. She does have a point and when she opens her palms and faces the tomb, I do the same, but I am not communing with a dead mortal and begging him for favors as many of the people around me. I address Allah whose presence is said to be as close to me as my jugular vein in the poetry of the Quran and I find in these words a universal quality which is how I interpret my faith. Know yourself and you will know your Lord. All our soul searching journeys are about this on some level. Knowing the Self.

Najma touches the tips of her fingers to her forehead and slightly bows her head. The she looks towards me and blows gently on my face just like my grandmother used to do after *namaz*, a gesture of blessing and goodwill that I find rather touching. And when we stand up and she hands me the plastic bag of rose petals to scatter on the saint's tomb. I gladly do my duty without being so defensive about it. Praying has relaxed me. And Najma as well. We don't speak much on the ride back to the house enjoying the comfort of silence like old friends.

*   *   *

The following day, Arshee's Land Rover honks at ten in the morning while I'm eating a breakfast of last night's *roti* smeared with marmalade in the living room, the only part of the house that is air conditioned. Arshee strides in with her hands on her hips.

"Come on you lazy creature! We haven't all day to waste!"

"What's the hurry? We're not going to Buckingham Palace are we? It's just your farm."

Arshee smacks me on the hand as I pretend to pout.

Maybe my joke is not that far off the mark. Arshee's digs might as well be a palace given all the decadence and perks of being married into a feudal land owning family with acres and acres of *kapas* or cotton fields. We drive past them in her SUV on our approach to the farm. A long dirt road driveway leads to a stately stone bungalow. Arshee highlights the farm's chief attributes from the open window pointing out their private mosque, *tandoor* clay oven, and a large well. Then we are enclosed in her plush air conditioned bedroom and I soon begin to realize that her definition of the word farm is very different from mine. This is no place for getting one's hands dirty milking the cows or cleaning out the chicken coop.

The house is full of servants roaming around from room to room leaving the mistress of the house blessedly free from chores. I'm starting to feel sorry for Arshee because the poor girl is so very lonely.

Part of it has to do with her marriage which appears strained because she had told me on the drive to the farm that at least I would have the option of getting divorced if things didn't work with my husband to be whereas she just has to put up with *jhagra*, all the bickering and fighting.

"What to do, *yaar*," says Arshee. "It is my fate."

"You could try to change it"

"Don't be such a silly! That's impossible!"

"It is not."

"It is so."

"No it's not!"

"Is so!"

"I give up! You are impossible to reason with."

I stretch out on her bed and turn sideways propped up by my elbow.

Arshee tosses me a silk cushion and assumes the same pose as though we are mirror images.

"You have thinking eyes," she says. "One of these days your head is going to explode if you don't give yourself a break."

"Ha ha. Very funny."

"You're a funny one and I like you too much."

She tickles me until I squeal for mercy.

"*Bas, bas*! Enough, enough!"

"Only on one condition."

Arshee has me pinned down at the arms. I'm in no position to fight back.

"Well what is it?"

"That you write me one letter every month from America and tell me all about your life."

"My dear Arshee. I should love to be able to write to you. You are so very writeable."

"*Pagli!*"

Arshee relaxes her grip and I'm free at last.

"Hey, I'm not that crazy! Miss come and visit my farm. Some of us have to work for a living you know!"

"Take that back!"

"OK. OK. I didn't mean it like that. But you know what I mean"

"Yes. Yes. I know. But it's not a bed of roses here either. Just the other day *Maasi* forgot to make the bed and just look at the way she has folded these clothes. I tell you some days I have had it up to here with these people!"

Arshee rubs her temples and then walks out of the bedroom yelling at the top of her voice for one of the servants. I glance at the laundry pile. A few odds and ends and some *kurtas* stacked on a sofa. Nothing out of order. But then again, Arshee and I don't seem to have the same set of standards coming as we do from two entirely different planets.

We spend the rest of the day watching a Bollywood flick on DVD. Arshee is a big fan of Rani Mukhurjee, the green eyed Bengali actress who co-stars with Shahrukh Khan in *Chalte, Chalte.* Arshee's cook, the *khansama*, brings us lunch, spicy *samosas* with cilantro chutney and mounds of rice with lamb curry and okra. We eat with our fingers as Arshee proceeds to sing along with the happy couple frolicking in the Greek isles where the film is shot.

I'm hoping to meet Arshee's husband in the evening and talk politics with a town mayor on the front lines of the Devolution Plan. *Devolution Plan.* I still can't say it with a straight face. It sounds so grandiose, this pseudo experiment with democracy. I've retained all the research files from Islamabad just in case they'll be useful in my future courses.

Boston. Graduate school. Lectures. Papers. Exams. That will be my life when I return to the States. I try to picture it, but all I can make out are the water thin images of a mirage. What I do know, my only known reality, is this moment, this silly movie, this farm which is so un-farmlike, this girl sitting beside me singing and humming, these curry stained fingers and that burp that just escaped.

The heaviness of the meal and the drone of Hindi on screen lull me to sleep. I wake up to the sensation of my legs being pulled every which way. Arshee smiles and pouts and envelopes me in a tearful hug. Stay. Stay with me, her eyes plead. You only just got here. She rings a little bell to summon a servant for tea. The DVD player is still on. Arshee sorts through a stack of movies and when she's unable to make a selection, she asks me to pick something out.

I have to go, I tell her. It's getting late. Arshee begs me to spend the night. Her mom won't mind. Really, she won't. Please stay. Just one night. Please. Please. Please. She keeps on insisting. But I can't give in. Her mother is expecting me back at her place. I don't want to be a rude guest. You are being rude and cruel too says the look in Arshee's eyes. She looks heartbroken.

The mysterious husband still hasn't returned and Arshee has no idea when or even if he'll be back to spend the night. Her shrug tells me that his absence is common practice. I feel so dreadfully sorry for this girl. What good is it to have this feudal lifestyle, a self made cocoon of privilege, when the price you pay for it is sheer lonesomeness.

It's almost dusk by the time I leave the farm. Arshee accompanies me on the ride back, her head resting on my shoulder like a sleepy infant. Our friendship has been fast and furious like a thunder shower. And nowhere else in Pakistan have I made friends with a woman so effortlessly. Maybe the reason why Arshee and I get along so well is because of her whole hearted acceptance of me just as I am. And I've reciprocated in equal measure. I intend to keep my promise and write to her in thin blue aerogrammes postmarked from Boston or Seattle all the way to Multan, Pakistan.

The letters will serve as a life line from one hemisphere to the other reminding me of the journey's soundtrack. Every journey has its own soundtrack. And a journey does not begin the moment we leave our doorstep, nor is it over when we have returned full circle. The journey begins much earlier in a nanosecond of thought or an image that inspires and its movements are like those of a symphony that is never really finished, but simply stops in interesting places. What we observe are the moments that shape our truth.

* * *

"Have some more chicken kebabs."

Pir Jee holds up a stainless platter filled with skewers of succulent boneless cubes marinated in yogurt and spices and cooked on an open fire. I put a hand on my rapidly ballooning tummy and politely refuse. No more kebabs. Pir Jee thrusts the platter in my direction, but I'm no longer tempted as any additional food will likely make my stomach explode and that will be the end of little old me and there will be no future, no graduation, no nothing. It's been weighing much more so on my mind, what I have to come home to, only because home is sitting right next to me, in the form of Adeel, Pir-Jee's Stateside cousin, who works at Microsoft and lives two miles away from my parents house in Seattle. It's a remarkable coincidence.

I'm watching Pir Jee making goofy faces at the younger children. Everyone is having a grand old time giggling and bouncing on the charpoy. Some of the older brothers and sisters are playing nearby in a patch of grass where a tire swing hangs on a tree branch. They urge me to join their game of hide and seek. I have no intentions of moving from this rope bed where I've been sitting for the past hour wondering how Pir Jee manages to remain so cheerful on a day so stiflingly hot that even the crows eyeing our picnic have called it quits from sheer exhaustion. There is absolutely no wind, only this oppressive Punjabi heat that feels like the inside of a six hundred and fifty degree oven.

Adeel's chatter distracts my thoughts and I'm back in Seattle, listening to him go on and on about the new Indian grocery store that has just opened up near the Microsoft campus where he can get all his spices, even hard to find items like *methi* or fenugreek seeds. Then he talks about his camping excursion to Mount Rainier where he was almost killed by a bear. He and his friend did not know they had to put away all the food and tie it up on trees. They didn't have to worry about bears in Pakistan.

Bears. *Methi*. Seattle. Multan.

My head is starting to spin. It's too much, all this mish mash of worlds colliding. The events of these last three days are beginning to swirl around like a merry-go-round that has lost all its novelty.

* * *

"What did you say?"

My rickshaw wallah is demanding a hundred Rupees to drop me at Tahira Aunty's house. It's a little over two US dollars, but extortion by local standards. I approach the next rickshaw and it's the same story. Then another and another. They're all competing against each other like school boys. I am the sought after prize in the ripping off the helpless tourist contest. A small platoon of men has gathered around me by now. Everyone wants to help. They do this by a great deal of arm waving, head shaking, and hollering all at the same time.

"Come with me! No, come with me!"

I'm being called in ten different directions. Maybe they take me for an octopus instead of a girl who's had a tiring eight hour bus journey from Multan to Lahore, the extra two and a half hours spent stranded on the highway waiting for a replacement tire when we had a puncture.

"Madam! This way! I am speaking very good English. I am BA from Punjab University. I do B-Commerce in chartered accountancy. Where you are going? No! Madam! Please! This way! This way!"

I break free from all the rickshaw wallahs and walk along on the busy road outside the bus terminal. Cars slow down and honk. Taxis prey in my footsteps like eagles scavenging for a meal. I'm being stubborn and cheap. I don't want to splurge on a cab. I don't want to ring Tahira Aunty and announce my arrival and hope that she will send me her car and driver which she probably won't. It's not so hard to flag a rickshaw. But now they're all full putt putting amid cauldrons of smoke. I keep on walking. The weight of my backpack and the three plastic bags in my hands are taking their toll. But I forge ahead like a martyr.

"Miss, Miss! I give you ride. Please you step inside. Please no walk."

Yet another rickshaw slows down and cruises beside me. Its driver is clean shaven and young. I ask him for the fare and he quotes the going rate. My luggage takes up the bulk of the peeling vinyl seat as I squeeze in and then we are off.

There are cars parked everywhere as Tahira Aunty's bungalow comes into view. Surely she cannot be having a party in the middle of the day. Something seems wrong. Horribly wrong. Nawaz comes up to the gate with a big smile on his face. How I've missed him. I feel like throwing my arms around his neck and squeezing him into a bear hug. But it would be the height of impropriety and I don't dare disturb the status quo when things look fragile enough as it is.

"Quran Khawani," Nawaz murmurs and goes on to tell me about the death of Tahira Aunty's sister's husband. The funeral already took place soon after he passed away yesterday morning. They're having a memorial service at the house where men and women gather to read the Quran in its entirety as a way of offering blessing to the recently departed. Most of the family is here. More are on their way.

"Khoob maza kar kay ayee ho."

Looks like you've had a blast. Nawaz smiles sweetly and carries my bags upstairs. I immediately turn on the air conditioner in my room while Nawaz scuttles down to the kitchen to bring me a snack so I can eat in privacy. He knows the last thing I want right now is to face all these strangers as they pummel me with questions about where I've been and what I've done and a zillion other inquiries that I'm in no mood to address. It's pointless to expend all that energy talking to people I shall probably never meet again. And then there are people that I want to talk to like Nawaz before I'm on that plane and out of his life forever.

Just one more week. I cannot bear to think of it. So I go on thinking that I'm going to stay like this always. That I'm going to keep on eating *daal chawal* with my fingers while sitting cross legged on this bed with the turquoise and yellow paisley patterned sheets, that the hum of traffic and dogs barking outside the window will continue night after night, that the dampness in my clothes will never go away, that my name will routinely be pronounced correctly, that the muezzin's call to prayer will remain a permanent fixture. It will all be over in a week. But I go on pretending otherwise.

It is eight PM by the time I've woken up from my nap. Just in time for dinner. I shower and change and go downstairs to the dining hall where the table is just being set. Nawaz has a helper tonight. He is tall and slim and wears a closely cropped beard. His eyes look rather sleazy.

"Sir," he pipes up as soon as another guy walks into the room. This one looks very familiar but I still cannot place him.

"It's you!" the new guy says.

"Yes, it's me," I reply. "And you are?"

"Don't tell me you've forgotten!"

I draw a complete blank. Tahira Aunty barges in and introduces me to her son Kamran. Of course. Kamran. I haven't seen him in fifteen years since he was a Pakistani foreign student living in my parents' basement in Seattle. Most of his time was spent at the college library or coffee shops so I never really saw much of him at home. But I gather he's done well for himself given his expensive looking clothes and the way his mother is gloating all over him as if he's the up and coming Donald Trump of Karachi.

"How very good of you to join us my dear. Do take a seat."

Tahira Aunty calls me to the dinner table. Her mood seems decidedly upbeat. Apparently the family death has been uplifting.

Kamran pulls out my chair in a gentlemanly way. He's wearing rather too much cologne.

"There she is! Our very own Marco Polo in the flesh!"

Rafiq Uncle is wearing his trademark white pajama and *kurta*. He looks a bit haggard with dark circles under his eyes. But he smiles at me and winks. I've missed his company. Most of all his wisecracks and the way he gangs up over his wife with affection and mischief.

"How was Multan?" asks Tahira Aunty.

"OK," I reply. "Not as atmospheric as Peshawar."

"I don't know what it is with you and the Frontier," she scoffs. "Such a bloody mess with all the fundos running around with their AK-47's and firebrand slogans. Our very own Dante's inferno if you ask me!"

"No no, you've got it all wrong," Rafiq Uncle counters. "The Frontier is the India of Kipling, the romance of empire. The Brits couldn't get enough of it. Fundos be damned!"

"Hear, hear!" I chorus.

Tahira Aunty rolls her eyes.

"Bollocks!"

Kamran looks back and forth between his parents and me as a silent spectator to our debate. He mops up the remaining mutton curry on his plate with some *naan* and picks up his cell phone to check messages. Then he stands by the doorway into the kitchen chatting with his driver whose eyes keep roving in my direction.

I've forgotten all about dinner now that I have Aunty and Uncle as a captive audience. The conversation veers towards the British. Even here, husband and wife are in stark disagreement.

He: The British presence in India was driven by commerce. Pure and simple. Their whole mission was to extract as large a share of revenues as possible from the jewel in the crown. They used politics as a tool. And they were very good at it exploiting long standing rivalries and factions among local rulers to gain a position of trust and foster divisions among the elites.

She: The British did a lot of good as rulers. They were not just common traders like the Dutch or the Portuguese. They gave us language, law, justice, roads, canals and railways not to mention a most excellent education system.

He: What about all the corruption, racism?

She: Compared to the level we have now, the Brits were positively angelic.

He: They made us cast off our clothes and wear suits and ties. They taught us how to socialize in clubs and play polo and cricket. They gave us gin fizz. In short, my dear, the Brits took us further and further away from our own culture. They made us look like aliens in our own land.

She: We are a colonized people. It's only natural that we will have split personalities.

He: We are divided amongst our own kind.

Indeed we are.

Tahira Aunty has moved on to desert, sumptuous brown balls of *gulab jamun* soaked in syrup. I take just one and then another and another. This stuff is lethal.

"I'd like to go to Wagah tomorrow," I say in between mouthfuls. "It would mean a lot to me."

Rafiq Uncle turns to me with a smile.

"And so you shall dear. And so you shall."

*   *   *

It could be a scene straight out of Monty Python. There are feathers and drums, tassels and military footwear. The soldiers are more than seven feet tall counting the huge fan-shaped headdresses they waggle at each other like peacock tails. For forty five minutes they high kick, stamp, march at full speed and shout their way through a choreographed routine known as the retreat ceremony that ends in the lowering of both flags and the slamming of the border gates.

Nawaz brings me a cup of chai and tells me the man at the tea stand suspects me of being *jasous*, an enemy spy from India. I take it as a compliment. My thoughts are mostly preoccupied in trying to figure out which soldier looks like an avatar of John Cleese.

I ought to see this pantomime ritual as something serious, even deadly – after all, here are two countries that have the potential to blow each other's brains out with a push of a button – but there is nothing here except for comedy, laced with tragedy.

The crowds on either side of the border cheer and clap like children watching a puppet show.

"Best wishes from India!" an older man shouts.

"Pakistan *zindabad*!" a yuppie yells.

As the Pakistan Rangers and the Border Security Forces of India conclude their performance, one of them winks at the other, a slight smile creeping across his lips that may just be part of this whole act. When I look towards the Indian side, most of the eyes are watching not just the soldiers, but the people themselves. There is intense curiosity and total recognition. One teenage girl looks straight at me. We're both wearing the *shalwar kameez* with color coordinated *dupattas*. She smiles and waves. I return her smile and wave back. I'm standing on the Pakistani side. I represent Pakistan. But this is no longer my home.

Five months of living and traveling in Pakistan have shown me what could have taken years to understand had I not taken the trouble of coming back. I've learned that I simply don't have the fortitude to live here anymore. You have to roll up your sleeves everyday and prepare to do battle with the elements. This is not to say that there is no struggling in America, but it's not the same as struggling in Pakistan. It becomes a question of individual personality and taste as to which type of struggle you prefer and where you choose to do it.

The ceremony has ended. The Indian and Pakistani guards stand with their backs turned to each other and pose for pictures. As luck would have it, I run out of film.

11
SONGS OF SINDH

Sindh province, October 2003

WE ARE HEADING NORTH up the National Highway, NH-5, into the dusty barren landscape of interior Sindh. Nadir tells me that the road we're on stretches from Karachi all the way to Torkham at the Afghan border. He shakes his head and laughs when I bring up Ghafoor, his Kalashnikov toting bodyguards and our numerous cups of tea along the Khyber Pass.

"Crazy people," Nadir admonishes. "Political Agent! Whatever possessed you to hook up with that lot?"

"We crazies need to stick together."

"Whatever you say," Nadir says with a weary sigh. "By the way, you know that Geeti and I are planning to go to Canada, right? In about a year or so, as soon as our immigration visas are finalized."

It comes as a total surprise since he hadn't mentioned it before. I presumed Nadir was a diehard Karachiite. The thought of leaving the city, of immigrating to Canada seems rather peculiar. Nadir tells me that he has been thinking about it for quite some time and it makes sense to go abroad and seek new opportunities in computer software.

"But there are so many people coming back right now," I say. "All the expats are returning home. It's a reverse migration. Why do you want to go the other way?"

"For the challenge," Nadir replies. "It is so easy to get complacent here."

"But what about all those Pakistanis who are settling back here?"
"Big fish in a small pond."

"What do you mean by that?"

"*Aree yaar,* it's so simple. Most of the expats coming back get to have little fiefdoms in Pakistan with their name and status. Out West, they're just keeping their heads afloat along with so many others. It takes a toll on the ego."

Nadir gives me a sly smile and accelerates to overtake a Toyota Corolla with tinted windows. I look out the window at the arid dusty landscape and for an instant I see a clear image of Nadir perched on a throne in a silk gown and turban with the Statue of Liberty rising in the background. My cousin is smiling and nodding and looks rather pleased. Is that why he's leaving one homeland for another? To reinvent himself on his own terms? Is this what happened to me?

"Baba, I need the toilet," Jaza whines from the backseat.

"She really needs to go," Geeti adds. "Where are your blasted tombs?"

"There are no tombs," I chime in. "Your dear husband is caught up in one of his fantasies again. There's no way we're going to see anything remotely interesting in this dustbowl. We might as well be on the moon!" I roll down my window and am instantly forewarned by a blast of hot wind pasting fine sand particles in my nose and hair.

"Here we are," Nadir says in a calm voice.

He brings the car to a stop alongside the road. It hugs the crest of a low ridge where stretching as far as the eye can see are masses of crumbly stone tombs that look like half eaten biscuits. Just seventeen miles due east of Karachi, we have arrived at a whole new planet. According to Nadir, the historic Chaukundi Tombs were built between the fifteenth and nineteenth centuries by some tribal people, most likely Baloch. There appears to be a whole city of tombs. They vary in height from five to fifteen feet. Some are like little houses with a rectangular base and a pyramid shaped roof supported by pillars. The most stunning thing about them is the intricate stone carvings that make each tomb look like an exquisite work of art. I've never seen anything quite like it.

"No one comes here anymore," Nadir says. "They're too afraid."

"Afraid of what?"

Nadir laughs. "Haven't you been reading the papers? Thieves, banditry, dacoits. Very bad people!"

He's being facetious, but I play along.

"Then what are we doing here? Are you trying to get us all killed or something?"

"I thought you wanted to see something *more authentic*," Nadir scoffs imitating my accent perfectly. "You were going on and on about it at dinner last night. Well here we are then little Miss-show-me-something-more-authentic-I'm-getting-tired-of-the-city. Feast your eyes on all this!"

Nadir extends both arms and spins like a dervish. His daughter Jaza who is standing nearby bursts into a fit of giggles.

"Just ignore your silly old Dad," I say and take Jaza's arm. "Come, let's find a discreet bathroom and check this place out."

"Wait, wait, I'm coming too!" Geeti shouts from the back seat of the car.

My camera keeps clicking in every direction. I take some close ups of Jaza's face juxtaposed against a border of rosettes. Most of the design work is geometric with squares, diamonds and zig zag patterns. Sometimes, I see images of horses and riders. According to the brief description in my guidebook, they are the graves of men, probably warriors. Some of the male graves are also decorated with a stone turban on top which reminds me of the kind I had seen in Turkey. Though Islamic art discourages representations of animals and people in favor of more abstract designs and calligraphy, these tombs suggest a more pagan influence that was in existence long before the advent of Muslim culture.

The cobalt sky is a sharp contrast against the beige-brown tombs. All around us the air is heavy with dust. Authentic Sindhi dust. I can almost taste it. The lighting is a bit too harsh for any decent shots, but I've gone shutter mad, moving from tomb to tomb, clicking at whatever catches my eye. I particularly like the illustrations of jewelry which mark the graves of women. There seems to be no sign of water, but there must be some form of irrigation to keep the valley below so green and fertile.

"Want to see more?"

Nadir catches up with us, arm and arm with Suraya Aunty, his mother, who manages to look impossibly chic in this sweltering desert heat with her oversized sunglasses and thin cotton *dupatta* tightly wound around her neck and adorning her head as protection from the blowing sand and dust.

"Yes sir!" I say. "More tombs please!"

"You ain't seen nothin' yet!"

We pile back in the car and proceed further up a dry and poor scrub land. Tiny, dilapidated villages come into view before we reach the desolate town of Banbhore near the mouth of the Indus River. Nadir tells us that it used to be a busy port that was taken over by Arab invaders, the first being Muhammad bin Qasim, who brought Islam into South Asia by the eighth century. Nearby is another ancient port, Gharo, which may have been founded by Alexander the Great. The museum there has artifacts of Greek pottery dating as far back as the first century BC. From Banbhore, we go up to Makli Hill which has millions of graves and is reputed to be the world's largest necropolis. It's a vast sprawling place, eerie and haunting and rather strange than sacred.

I don't like it as much as Chaukundi whose contained intimacy was far more pleasant.

Jaza leads me into a tomb with a circular archway and curving walls. Luckily, I see him before she does. A tall thin man with brown-black skin. His *shalwar* is undone. I immediately move away and keep a firm hand on Jaza's back steering her toward safety toward a small circle of onlookers watching a small monkey dance to the beat of drums.

"What's wrong?" Nadir asks as he breaks from the circle and approaches us.

"Nothing, nothing."

"Your face is all flushed," Geeti says touching my cheeks and forehead.

"Is it?" I, uhh, I guess I'm not used to this Sindhi sun."

"Are you sure you're OK?" Geeti asks.

"Yes, of course. Just a bit hot, that's all. Can we go somewhere else to cool off?"

"Not really," Nadir says with a slight smile. "But we'll make one last stop before heading back. You can't come all this way and not see Thatta!"

*   *   *

It's about sixty miles from Karachi and in the old days, it may have been the site of the ancient city of Pattala where Alexander rested his troops before his near fatal march across the Makran Desert. Thatta's history goes back at least two thousand years. In its heyday, it was a prosperous trading post famous for wood carving and cotton-weaving as well as a refuge for saints and scholars. During the Middle Ages, Thatta's stature grew as Sindh's capital and the city absorbed the cultural and architectural influences of four successive Muslim dynasties, the most prominent were the Mughals whose rule lasted until the mid-eighteenth century. The Mughal emperor Shah Jahan, visionary architect of the Taj Mahal, left another historic landmark by commissioning a mosque to thank the people of Thatta for their warm welcome when he resided here as a youth.

We reach Shah Jahan's mosque by driving through Thatta's hodgepodge commercial strip, lined with sportswear clothing, juice stalls, PCO phone booths and internet cafes. Nadir parks the car under the shade of an old juniper tree. Just outside the mosque's entrance, I am besotted by some unusual glass bangles that are hexagon in shape with rich earthy colors. They are what the poor Sindhi women wear, beggars and sweepers. I buy a dozen bangles to adorn my wrist. The village girl who sells them to me smiles bashfully as I hand her a hundred rupee note and walk away. It is not enough. It is never enough.

The most unusual thing about Thatta's mosque is its lack of minarets. Instead, there are a series of domes, about a hundred according to Nadir, that are laid out in such a way that the imam's voice leading the prayers can be heard anywhere in the mosque without the need of a loudspeaker. Arcades of red brick arches highlighted with bands of white surround the courtyard. As most Mughal buildings are constructed with marble and sandstone, I presume the use of brick must be a practical matter which nonetheless enhances the mosque's esthetics by presenting a striking visual contrast to the glazed tile work with its soothing color schemes of turquoise blue and rose. One wall is patterned with black and white stripes, a remarkably contemporary look for a structure built in the sixteenth century.

There are men napping in the cool inner chambers, their faces partially covered with the material of a shawl or turban. We find an empty spot to say the *asr namaz,* the late afternoon prayers. Suraya Aunty, Geeti, Jaza and I stand next to each other shoulder to shoulder while Nadir stands a few feet in front of us.

Allahu Akbar.

We fold our arms over our chests.

Allahu Akbar.

We put our hands on our knees and bend.

Allahu Akbar

We touch our foreheads on the bare floor.

Allahu Akbar.

We sit down.

Allahu Akbar.

We stand up.

The prostration is repeated four times. Our movements remain synchronized, the choreography of praying simple and joyous. I feel a sense of peace. There is no need to question, to ponder, to debate. At least for the moment, which like all moments is fleeting, but I live in it just for half hour or so unencumbered and whole.

No one talks much on the drive back to Karachi. I fall asleep most of the way home.

MAP OF PAKISTAN

Urdu/English Glossary

Aankhon – eyes

Aao – come, this way

Aayista – slowly, slow down

Afsos – sadness, sorrow

Ajnabee –foreigner, stranger, outsider

Aloo – potato

Aloo parathas – Fried bread filled with potatoes

Almari - closet

Amroot – guava

Bachi – young girl

Baingan – eggplant

Bazaar - marketplace

Bedis – thin hand rolled cigarettes

Beti – daughter

Bhel puris – popular South Asian snack consisting of puffed rice balls dipped in a tangy tamarind sauce

Bhindi – okra

Biryani – Rice dish made with mutton, chicken, seafood and or vegetables

Burqa – cloak like garment that covers a woman from head to toe

Chador – thin cotton shawl

Chaliswah – fortieth day of mourning

Chalo – let's go; common

Chapli kebab – minced beef patty popular in Pakistan and Afghanistan

Chappals – flip flops or sandals

Chappati – unleavened flatbread

Charas - hash

Chawal - rice

Chee –gross, yuck

Chicoo – tropical fruit that looks like kiwi, also known as *sapota*

Chit – note

Chota hazri – early morning tea or light breakfast; adopted by the
　　　　British during the Raj

Chowk – traffic roundabout

Chukidar – guard or gatekeeper

Churidar – skin tight trousers scrunched at the ankles

Daal – South Asian lentils

Dadi – paternal grandmother

Daroo – homemade moonshine alcohol mainly produced in rural areas

Dholak – South Asian drum used at weddings and festivities

Dil – heart

Dua - prayers

Dulan – South Asian bride

Dupatta – Long, rectangle shaped South Asian scarf to accompany
　　　　the *shalwar kameez*

Durrie – thin flat woven rug

Faqir – vagrant, bum, also poor

Ghar – house

Gharara – voluminous skirt consisting of two separate panels for each
　　　　leg; also known as *ghagra*

Ghost – meat

Goondas – thugs

Gulab jamon – popular South Asian desert equivalent to donuts immersed in warm sweet syrup

Haina – isn't that so?

Haldi – tumeric

Hartal – strike

Havelis – Historic South Asian mansions

Hazara – minority ethnic group in Afghanistan and Pakistan with Mongolian lineage

Hijra – South Asian transsexual, also known as eunuch

Hijrah – migration; a reference to the Prophet Muhammad's flight from Mecca to Medina to escape persecution in 622 AD; also used the starting point for the Islamic calendar

Hindko – language spoken by a Hazara

Hungama –noise, commotion, boisterousness

Iftar – post sunset meal to break the fast during Ramadan

Inshallah – Arabic term for God willing

Izzat – respect, honor

Jaldi – hurry up

Jasous - spy

Jelabis – Indian style funnel cakes that are extremely sweet and sticky with syrup and usually eaten while warm

Jhagra – fight, argument

Ji – formal term for yes

Jinn – evil spirit common in South Asian folklore

Junglee – wild, savage

Kapas - cotton

Karhai – hand crafted embroidery

Kasam – promise, oath

Khajoor – dates

Khalas – maternal aunts

Khana – food

Khansama – cook or chef

Kheer – South Asian rice pudding

Khusa – Handmade artisanal shoes made in India and Pakistan with leather and textile and embellished with brass nails, shells, mirrors, beads; also known as *mojari*

Kismet – fate, destiny

Kolhapuri – hand crafted South Asian open toe sandals usually made out of buffalo hide

Kulfi – South Asian ice cream

Kurta – long loose tunic

Lakh – monetary amount equivalent to 100,000

Lassi – South Asian yogurt drink made either sweet or salty

Lengha – long dressy skirt richly embellished and worn at formal
occasions and weddings

Loo – British term for bathroom

Maasi – maid servant

Maghrib – sundown prayer

Markaz – embassy

Masjid – mosque

Maza – fun, enjoyment; also taste

Mazar – tomb

Mehman – guest

Methi – fenugreek

Milad – religious ceremony to commemorate the Prophet Muhammad's
birthday

Mir – Princely ruler

Mohabbat – romantic love

Mohajir – Indian Muslim migrant who came to Pakistan after Partition

Mujahideen – resistance fighters during the Soviet occupation of
          Afghanistan

Naan – Puffy South Asian bread

Namaz – prayers

Nani – maternal grandmother

Nazim – city or district level magistrate equivalent to mayor

Neem – evergreen tree common in the Subcontinent with many
          medicinal uses. Also known as *margosa*

Nikkhah – religious ceremony in a Muslim wedding that declares the
          couple as man and wife

Nimboo pani – lemonade

Niqab – face veil usually in thick black cloth

Oopur – upstairs

Paan – South Asian concoction made from betel leaf, lime and
          various nuts eaten as a digestive

Pakora – deep fried dumpling made from chick pea flour

Pagli – crazy, wacko, also used as a term of endearment

Paharon – mountains

Palak – spinach

Paneer – South Asian cheese

Partition – the division of British India in August 1947 that created the independent nation states of India and Pakistan

Pera – a flattened ball of dough

Pir – South Asian term for a spiritual/religious figure commonly associated with Sufism; equivalent to saint

Puran poli – Indian style crepe with a sweet lentil filling

Pyar – love, affection

Quran Khawani – group reading of the Quran following a death

Raat ki rani – fragrant shrub with tiny white flowers common in the tropics that is similar to Jasmine; literally means Queen of the Night

Rabab – bowed string instrument

Rani – queen

Rickshaw – essential mode of urban transport in South Asia; a three wheeled motorized vehicle for hire

Rickshaw wallah – person who drives the rickshaw

Roti – South Asian tortilla

Saab – equivalent to sir; used for the elderly and authority figures

Salaam – common greeting in Arabic speaking and Muslim countries equivalent to hi/hello; salutation meaning peace

Samosas – stuffed savory pastries filled with spicy potatoes, onions, peas, lentils, ground lamb or chicken

Shabash – well done as in a form of praise

Shadi – wedding or marriage

Shalwar kameez – Traditional South Asian outfit consisting of knee length tunic with side slits and draw string baggy trousers

Shukria – thank you

Souq – Middle Eastern marketplace

Sunno – listen up

Such – truth

Tandoor – clay oven

Tehsildar – village administrator

Tiffin – stainless steel lunch box

Tikka (used with chicken) – chunks of boneless chicken marinated in yogurt and spices

Tikka – ornamental jewelry that hangs in the middle of the forehead and attached with pins along the part in the middle of the hair; also spelled as *teeka*

Yaar – friend, pal, buddy

Zabaan – language; also means tongue

SELECTED BIBLIOGRAPHY
FICTION AND NON FICTION

Ahmad, Salman, *Rock and Roll Jihad: A Muslim Rock Star's Revolution*, Free Press, 2010

Ahmed, Akbar, *Jinnah, Pakistan and Islamic Identity: The Search for Saladin*, Routledge, 1997

Bach, Paul, Brian, *The Grand Trunk Road: From the Front Seat*, Indus, 2000

Banik, Allen: *Hunza Land: The Fabulous Health and Youth Wonderland of the World*, Whitehorn Publishing, 1960

Hanif, Mohammed, *A Case of Exploding Mangoes*, Vintage, 2009

Hamid, Mohsin, *Moth Smoke*, Picador, 2001

Jalal, Ayesha, *The Pity of Partition: Manto's Life, Times and Work across the India-Pakistan Divide*, Princeton University Press, 2013

Jalal, Ayesha, *The Sole Spokesperson: Jinnah, the Muslim League and the Demand for Pakistan*, Cambridge University Press, 1994

Keay, John, *The Gilgit Game: The Explorers of the Western Himalayas 1865-95*, Oxford University Press, 1994

Khan, Asghar, *The Pakistan Experience: State and Religion*, Vanguard Books, 1985

Khan, Aslam, Uzma, *Tresspassing*, Picador, 2005

Khan, Yasmin, *The Great Partition: The Making of India and Pakistan*, Yale University Press, 2008

Lari, Yasmin, *The Dual City: Karachi During the Raj*, Oxford University Press, 1997

Manto, Hasan, Sadat, *Black Milk*, Translated from the Urdu by Hamid Jalal, Sang-e-Meel Publications, 1997

Shamsie, Kamila, *Kartography*, Mariner Books, 2004

Suleiri, Sara, *Meatless Days*, University of Chicago, 1991

ACKNOWLEDGMENTS

First and foremost, I would like to thank Kenneth Shear and my Booktrope team members for taking on this project with such enthusiasm. I appreciate all your support.

I am also thankful beyond measure for all the angels who made this journey happen and vouched for my safety by guiding me along the way with wisdom and compassion:

Special thanks for Hassan Abbas for scribbling on a grubby paper napkin in a Boston pub which ultimately took me to the rooftop of the world. Kudos to Major Salim Malik for transporting me on the fabulous Karakoram Highway in such royal comfort and for providing the adventure of a lifetime. For my aunt Farida in Seattle, I am grateful for the gift of Lahore. To all my colleagues at the International Crisis Group in Islamabad, thank you for bringing me on board and letting me witness history in the making. I am also grateful to all my Isloo friends and acquaintances for giving me a potent taste of local culture and for many laughs. To my cousin Nadir and his family in Karachi, many thanks for putting up with all my annoying questions. For Kamla Aunty, may you never lose your sense of style and elegance that is inseparable from Karachi. For Abdul Ghafoor Shah and Anwar, thank you for letting me brave the Frontier and come away unscathed. For Arshee, our friendship is sealed forever. I will never forget you or your slice of Multan. For Nawaz, I owe thanks for all your culinary masterpieces and for that incredible motorcycle ride along the GT road.

For my esteemed Professor, Ayesha Jalal, thank you for inspiring me with your intellect and grace. To my parents, Ammi and Abboo, you continue to humble me with your collective strength and your power of faith. I am particularly indebted to my father for sharing his memories about Dizzy Gillespie that ignited the spark to write this book. I also want to thank John Mifsud and the Jack Straw Writers Program in Seattle for letting my voice be heard. To my dear husband, Anthony, thank you as always for believing in me and for tolerating all my shortcomings. To my cousin Omar in New York, many many thanks for making my ideas see the light of day. Finally, to my precious Azeem, thank you for reminding Mama each and every day of what truly matters.

MEET MALIHA MASOOD,
AUTHOR OF *DIZZY IN KARACHI*

I don't really see myself as a writer. Certainly not a travel writer. Although the subjects I tend to write about the most have to do with places, culture, and travel, not just as a destination, but also a state of mind. Writing a book is hard work and I do it not out of love, but out of necessity. The stories are just too good to keep entirely to myself. I feel compelled to share my experiences with the world in order to add a perspective that is different and offbeat, something that makes you rethink what you know and maybe even spark a new dialogue.

I'm not big on finding all the answers. My goal is to keep on questioning and try to find better questions than answers so that we are not complacent. I can't stand know it alls. There's always a hidden element to every story and what we see on the surface is never ever the full picture. I like the stories lurking in between. I call them shadowlands. And that's what I attempt to convey through my writings. Though my work is nonfiction, I strive to make it interesting and relevant so that when you read it, you might find it like a novel and be thoroughly transported to another reality, in the comfort of your pajamas.

My first book was about the Middle East where I backpacked across Egypt, Jordan, Lebanon, Syria and Turkey for one year, mostly by myself. It was an amazing adventure and I wrote about it to humanize a part of the world riddled with fear and suspicion. I feel the same way about Pakistan which is a lot more personal because it happens to be my childhood home. Now that you've read this book, it must be pretty clear that I have a big complex when it comes to Pakistan. Because I cannot disassociate myself from all its loaded meanings. It's a roller coaster of emotions. Shame, embarrassment, pride, love, nostalgia, anger, confusion all the same time at the mere utterance of Pakistan.

I had to come to terms with it. Which is why I went back. And then I just fell into one crazy adventure after another. Almost as if someone else was orchestrating this journey and all I had to do was tag along on the ride and be open to the experience. And in so doing, I slipped through the cracks and unearthed my shadowlands. What I came away with is not what I was expecting to find. I never really found a sense of home in Pakistan because it was no longer the home I had grown up in. What did bind me to the country, were the people I met there, not my own family, but total strangers who welcomed me with open arms and allowed me a precious glimpse of their world. I couldn't have written this book without them.

And so my story is not entirely my own. It is a collective tale of encounters that at first seemed random, but upon further reflection, were meant to be. My take on all of this is very subjective and far from authoritative. I trust the reader to reach his or her own conclusions, but whatever they are, I hope there has been a shift in perspective from the one you started out with and that you found me to be good travel mate, infuriating perhaps, but far from boring.

DISCUSSION QUESTIONS FOR
DIZZY IN KARACHI

1. What is the significance of the title?

2. How does this book compare to other books about Pakistan? In what ways is it different, how is it the same?

3. What are some themes that are specific to this book? Are there any themes that are universal?

4. What is the book's tone? How does it shape the narrative?

5. What is the author striving for, what is she hoping to learn, to discover on this journey?

6. What is the role of the past in informing the present? How does this it play out in the book?

7. Why is culture important? How does the author negotiate her cultural duality?

8. What does homeland mean? Is it strictly about a place? What other factors represent our concept of home?

9. Where does the author stand on politics? Can Pakistan be entirely explained by its political landscape?

10. How does class affect social mores in Pakistan? Is it a class ridden society? What about the role of religion? Of language?

11. How does this book challenge stereotypes about Pakistan? Which ones are broken? Which are not?

12. What role does gender play in Pakistan? Does the author transgress gender barriers?

13. What is the author's take on travel? Is she a reckless traveler?

14. Which of the book's characters made an impression? Why?

15. What changes at the end? For the author? For the reader?

To access more information, including a curriculum guide for educators and a discussion forum for bloggers, please visit the website at
www.dizzyinkarachi.com

To contact the author for speaking requests or presentations, please email
dizzyinkarachi@gmail.com.

MORE GREAT READS FROM BOOKTROPE

Tulip Season **by Bharti Kirchner** (Mystery) Mitra searches for her best friend, a domestic-violence counselor, who has disappeared from her Seattle home. Following the trail, Mitra is lured to India, and lands in a web of life-threatening intrigue where she can't be sure of Kareena's safety—or her own.

Bumbling into Body Hair – A Transsexual's Memoir **by Everett Maroon** (Memoir) A comical memoir about a klutz's sex change, showing how a sense of humor—and true love—can triumph over hair disasters, and even the most crippling self-doubt.

Write for the Fight **by Tess Hardwick and Tracey M. Hansen** (Memoir) Heartwarming, funny and thought-provoking, Write for the Fight reveals the personal memories, fears and dreams of 13 writers as they reflect on defining moments of the past and dream of possibilities for the future.

… and many more!

Sample our books at:
www.booktrope.com

Learn more about our new approach to publishing at:
www.booktropepublishing.com

CPSIA information can be obtained at www.ICGtesting.com
Printed in the USA
BVOW07s0122110913

330824BV00001B/10/P